To all the faithful workers in the field
of Russian liturgical singing.

Johann von Gardner

RUSSIAN CHURCH SINGING

VOLUME I
Orthodox Worship and Hymnography

Translated by
VLADIMIR MOROSAN

ST. VLADIMIR'S SEMINARY PRESS
Crestwood, New York
1980

Library of Congress Cataloging in Publication Data

Gardner, Johann von.
  Russian church singing.

  German translation has title: System und Wesen
des russischen Kirchengesanges.
  Includes bibliographical references.
  CONTENTS: v. 1. Orthodox worship and
hymnography.
  1. Church music—Orthodox Eastern Church,
Russian—History and criticism. I. Title.
ML3060.G22   783'.02'61947   79-27480
ISBN 0-913836-56-7

Publication of this volume was greatly facilitated by assistance from
The Russian Brotherhood Organization, Philadelphia, Pennsylvania

PRINTED IN THE UNITED STATES OF AMERICA
BY
ATHENS PRINTING COMPANY
461 Eighth Avenue
New York, NY 10001

RUSSIAN CHURCH SINGING

Contents

Translator's Preface

In the autumn of 1973, while doing research in Russian liturgical singing under the auspices of a Thomas J. Watson Foundation fellowship, I had the good fortune of visiting Dr. Johann (Ivan Alekseevich) von Gardner at his home in Munich, Germany. It was at that memorable meeting that I first found out about the existence of the yet unpublished work *Russian Liturgical Singing: Its Essence, Structure, and History.*

At the time I met Professor Gardner, I had already undergone the unpleasant and frustrating experience so familiar to all prospective researchers in the field of Russian Orthodox liturgical singing: not only the total lack of reference materials in the English language, but also, the virtual inaccessibility of the numerous pre-Revolutionary reference works in Russian (even if one happened to have, as I did, the good fortune of knowing the language). The discovery of a major work by the most prominent scholar in this field outside the USSR was, therefore, very exciting. A few hours spent with Professor Gardner, during which he openly shared with me the immeasurable depths of his knowledge and expertise, served to fuel my expectations concerning the vast treasures that must be contained in his book.

The work, however, just like its pre-Revolutionary predecessors, was not available: for two years already it had lain on the shelves of a Russian émigré publishing concern, and very little progress was being made towards its publication. It was at that time that the idea of an English translation first entered my mind. The original Russian version, when published, would have more of an historical, rather than an immediate practical significance; an English translation, on the other hand, would serve an immediate purpose in several different quarters.

The fate of Russian Orthodox liturgical singing is a sad illustration of the fragile dependence that certain kinds of art have on political and historical conditions. Traditionally fulfilling its role as an immanent and inseparable aspect of church worship, Russian liturgical singing never fully developed the same degree of artistic and ideological independence from the Church as was achieved by Western sacred music. Consequently, the same repercussions that were suffered by the Russian Church after the Communist takeover of 1917 befell Russian liturgical singing. All artistic performance of the repertoire ceased, and singing in churches, to the extent it was allowed, restricted itself to a preservation of the status quo. The young but burgeoning academic descipline of Russian liturgical musicology, which by the end of the nineteenth century had already succeeded in inspiring a veritable renaissance of nationalistic choral composition along traditional liturgical lines, also suffered a painful interruption, the broken threads of which are only tentatively being gathered today by a new generation of Soviet scholars. In the West, the music, after enjoying a brief stint of popularity in the 1920's and 30's, largely in the form of English adaptations for Protestant church use, has now fallen into virtual oblivion. As a result, the burden of serving as caretakers for the nearly thousand-year-long tradition of Russian liturgical singing has fallen on the shoulders of the ever-shrinking Russian emigration, which, except in a few isolated instances, has proven to be academically and musically unprepared to fulfill such a task.*

At the same time, Russian Orthodox liturgical singing has continued to attract, in however small numbers, an unceasing stream of "adoptive parents," Western scholars as well as performers, who have been drawn either by its rich but still obscure historical heritage, replete with undeciphered notations, unexplored sources, and untranscribed manuscripts, or by the sonorities of its serene melismatic chants and majestic choral settings. No less than a dozen theses and dissertations on the subject have appeared at American and Western European universities within the past several decades. Ensembles such as the Johannes Damascenus Choir and the Romanos-Chor (both of Essen, Germany), the Yale Russian Chorus (of New Haven, Connecticut), the Philharmonic Chorus (of Madison, Wisconsin), the University of Illinois Russian Choir (of Urbana, Illinois), all composed primarily of non-Russians, have devoted a major portion of their performing efforts to Russian liturgical singing.

Equally as important has been the establishment and growth of Orthodox Christianity on American and Western European soil:

---

* In the academic field Johann v. Gardner and the late Alfred Swan have been virtually the only scholars to have made substantial contributions.

In the practical field of musical performance one may single out such figures as Nicholas Afonsky and Boris Ledkovsky, both deceased, and the still active Serge Jaroff and Evgenii Evetz.

the parishes established by the Church of Russia have naturally preserved the choral tradition of the Mother-Church, and even parishes coming from Greek or Syrian traditions of monodic chant have in some instances adopted Russian choral singing under the influence of the prevailing choral milieu of the West. With time, of course, these various ethnic groups will become welded into an American Orthodox Church and will develop a native American Orthodox tradition of liturgical singing; but in the meantime they are contenting themselves with maintaining the musical heritage of the past by means of translations, adaptions, and imitative compositions and arrangements.

Just as the author of this work dedicated his original Russian version "to all the faithful workers in the field of *Russian* liturgical singing," so this translation is dedicated to all of the aforementioned groups of workers in the field of all Orthodox liturgical singing in the Western world.

This work contains the ground-laying essentials necessary for any prospective worker in this field; depending on his orientation and needs, however, every reader will find that it offers special rewards for the particular area of interest to him. The neophyte choir director and the convert to Orthodoxy will find an explanation of the nature and structure of Orthodox services and definitions of types and categories of hymns. The practicing choral conductor will deepen his theoretical knowledge regarding the history and function of singing in the liturgy. The prospective scholar will not only find a comprehensive historical background upon which to build his research, but will also be guided towards some of the most pressing problems that require additional investigation. The prospective composer of Orthodox hymns will become aware of the rich heritage and tradition that have always guided the best creative artists of the past.

To the English reader this work will in many ways serve the same function as Rev. Dmitrii Razumovskii's *Church Singing in Russia* did for Russian readers almost exactly one hundred years ago: it will uncover a vast storehouse of previously unknown information and will stimulate new creative efforts and scholarship.

In translating this work for the English-speaking reader, a number of editorial modifications had to be made. The translator added numerous explanatory notes defining concepts and terms that may have proven to be unfamiliar to the Western reader. Following the wishes of the author, the structure of the first volume was reorganized to conform with the previously published German edition: *System und Wesen des russischen Kirchengesanges* (Wiesbaden: Otto Harrassowitz, 1976); thus, the chapter dealing with the structure of

Orthodox services nas been added from the German version. Also upon the request of the author, the preface has been extensively revised with the English reader in mind. The arrangement and division of chapters has been altered somewhat: the most major change involved the transferring of the annotated bibliography from its original position as Chapter 2 to an appendix at the end of the last volume. Particular care has been exercised to employ the most correct and current terminology and text translations: in nearly all cases anglicized Greek terms commonly found in Western scholarly usage have been employed, supplemented by the original Greek and Slavonic equivalents. For technical reasons, terms and titles originally in Church Slavonic have been rendered in modern Cyrillic characters but in old orthography; Russian terms and titles have been rendered in new orthography.

I wish to express my sincere gratitude to the following individuals: Ivan Schian, Marina Ledkovsky, and David Drillock, who helped to conceive and inspire this translation; His Grace, Bishop Laurus, of the Holy Trinity Monastery in Jordanville, New York, who supplied a copy of the original MS; John Erickson, of St. Vladimir's Seminary Press, who provided invaluable advice; and my wife Zhenia, who not only put up with endless hours of typing, but also consented to proofread the translated manuscript afterwards.

—*Vladimir Morosan,*
November, 1978

Author's Preface

The present work is intended as an aid to those who feel the necessity of gaining a deeper understanding of the liturgical singing of the Russian Orthodox Church, not only in its present-day practical forms, but also in its theoretical essence and thousand-year history. Such an understanding will enable the person interested in pursuing Orthodox liturgical singing in either its scholarly or its practical aspect to recognize the appropriate direction in which to travel, ensuring that liturgical singing will maintain its churchly character as an immanent part of the liturgy itself.

Since the Church in a sense is timeless, existing both outside of time and encompassing all of time, its singing also must preserve the traditions of the past while maintaining a link with the present. Above all, the singing of the Church must never stray from its central essence: the liturgy. It must avoid at all costs the tendency to pursue exclusively aesthetic or personal, subjective goals. Only a thorough knowledge of the entire system and history of Orthodox liturgical singing will enable this middle ground to be found.

In its present form this work represents the summation and thorough reworking of my lectures on the history and essence of Russian liturgical singing read between 1954 and 1972 in the Slavic division of the Faculty of Philosophy at the University of Munich. In this work I have attempted to summarize the present state of knowledge in those fields, as well as to give a critical appraisal to some of the views and conclusions of earlier researchers in the area of Russian liturgical singing.

One of my primary concerns, especially in the first part of the work, was to organize in an orderly fashion the vast amount of information concerning the system of Orthodox liturgical singing. While it was not possible to enter deeply into questions of a purely liturgical or liturgico-archeological nature, the historical aspect was included to the extent necessary for a thorough treatment of our subject and the avoidance of certain errors that may result from an insufficient historical understanding.

Special attention was directed to the proper use of various expressions and terms. Frequently writers of the past, as well as individuals working in the field of liturgical singing today, do not employ correct terminology, betraying a certain lack of erudition and expertise on their part.

In defining our subject the first question that had to be answered was: What is liturgical singing in essence? In spite of the apparent clarity of the question, the answers one hears in response to it are usually not based on any clearly defined premises and, as a result, vary greatly from individual to individual. A great majority, not only among the laity but also among choir directors, choir singers and clergy, believe that liturgical singing belongs entirely to the field of music. In their view church singing is choral music distinguished from secular music only by the fact that the former is performed in church during worship services and contains a sacred liturgical text (in the predominant liturgical language of a given parish: Greek, Church Slavonic, English, etc.).

Such an understanding of liturgical singing, however, is extremely superficial and by no means gives an accurate appraisal of our subject. In the course of the first part of this work it will become clear that Orthodox liturgical singing represents an entirely distinct sphere in the area of the liturgical arts, having its own principles of organization and aesthetic requirements.

In speaking of liturgical singing we shall be considering not only the melodic renditions of given liturgical texts, but also the overall manifestation of the musical element in the Orthodox liturgy and, specifically, in the liturgical practice of the Russian Church. An important aspect in the study of the system of Russian church singing is the examination of different styles of performance, a subject that is closely tied to both practical liturgics and liturgical archeology. At first glance it seems superfluous to speak of different styles of performance, since the singing of the Russian Orthodox Church today is almost exclusively of one style, i.e. that of choral polyphony. However it is necessary to recognize that various styles of performance are an integral part of the prescriptions contained in the Typikon (or Rule) governing the services of the entire Eastern Orthodox Church. Seen from that perspective the choral singing employed in the Russian Church today becomes only a limited and selective adaptation of those more general rules.

In this connection it must be pointed out that while the order of worship, i.e. the order governing the sequence of the liturgical texts, liturgical actions etc., is the same for all national branches of the Orthodox Church (discounting slight differences between the Slavic and Greek traditions), the liturgical singing of each branch is different—in melodic content, in prevalent styles of execution, and even in the manner of vocal production. The reasons for these differences lie in a multitude of historical and cultural influences, the detailed examination of which lies outside the scope of the present work. This work will focus only on the system and history of Russian liturgical singing; the singing of other Orthodox churches and of non-Orthodox Christian denominations will be mentioned only on occasion by way of comparison.

A major aspect of our study will consist of examining the manner in which melodic and all sonorous material in general is organized in Orthodox services: the musical and melodic systems of chants (распевы) that form the basis for the canonical singing of the Russian Church. Thus we enter into an area of historical musicology or, rather, a special branch of it: Russian liturgical musicology.

Since this field may not be familiar to many of our readers, it is necessary to say a few words about what it concerns. By its nature, Russian liturgical musicology is what the Germans call a *Grenzwissenschaft*, a "borderline discipline," i.e. one that draws upon many other disciplines and contributes to them as well, but does not coincide exactly with any of them. Below are listed some of the primary fields with which our subject will be concerned:

The general history and theory of music must be considered. Specifically, the history of Byzantine music (early and late) and ancient Greek musical theory, traces of which can be discerned in Byzantine church singing, will be considered. In addition, the system and history of Gregorian chant, the canonical singing of the Roman Catholic Church, provide an overall context that is likely to be more familiar to the Western reader. It must be remembered that much of the initial development of the Gregorian system occurred before the ultimate separation of the Eastern and Western churches in 1054. Moreover, Roman Catholic influence became quite strong in the Russian Church during the seventeenth century, especially affecting the musical thinking of Orthodox in the western regions of Russia that belonged at the time to Poland and Lithuania. Beginning with the mid-seventeenth century, Russian liturgical singing begins to parallel very closely the history and development of Western European music, maintaining at the same time a distinct identity and historical course.

The history of the Russian Church and of its relationships with

other Orthodox and non-Orthodox churches constitutes the framework within which the entire development of liturgical singing took
place, and many events of a broader historical nature affected developments in liturgical singing.

Philology and linguistics must be considered because liturgical
singing is very tightly connected with the development of the Russian
(Slavonic) language over the centuries. In the very early stages of
the Russian Church one is confronted with the problem of translations of Greek texts into Slavonic and with the application of those
translations to singing in a certain manner. In later periods the
pronunciation of the liturgical language had a marked effect upon
liturgical singing: the necessity of vocalizing certain phonemes, of
tailoring melodies to given metric-syllabic structures, of accommodating changing conventions of text accentuation, etc. inevitably
affected the musical aspect of liturgical singing.

The closely related fields of *paleography and semeiography,*
which deal with ancient literary and musical notations, provide the
clues by which we can decipher and understand ancient written monuments of liturgical singing. While it cannot be expected that a rank-
and-file parish choir director will have special expertise in these fields,
some knowledge of ancient notations and their principles should be
part of one's general education in the area of liturgical singing, to say
nothing of the prospective specialist in the field. The present work
gives only the most basic information for the understanding of
ancient musical manuscripts and their notation; those who wish to
explore further this fascinating field are referred to specialized literature given in the bibliography. It is unfortunate that in the sixty-plus
years since the Russian Revolution of 1917 virtually no new works have
appeared on this subject outside of Russia; interested researchers
must still attempt to obtain necessary materials from archives and
manuscript repositories in the Soviet Union through inter-library
exchanges.

Finally, the field of *liturgics,* both in its practical (rubrical)
aspect and in its historical aspect, is crucial to the understanding of
the forms and the styles of performance of liturgical singing. Since
liturgical singing has always been an immanent aspect of the liturgy
itself, it is self-evident that developments and changes in the order of
the liturgy have had an effect on the forms of singing. On the other
hand, the evolution of liturgico-musical forms has had an effect upon
the liturgical order, particularly during the last two centuries. As an
aid to the non-Orthodox reader a special chapter has been added
in both the German and the English editions of this work, dealing
specifically with the structure of various Orthodox services.

As recently as the third quarter of the nineteenth century, Russian liturgical musicology did not exist as a distinct scholarly discipline, and many in fact questioned the possibility of its existence. The study and knowledge of liturgics as well as liturgical singing were limited to a practical mastery of the church Typikon and its prescribed forms. Such a level of mastery was considered essential but sufficient for clergy and choir directors alike. Indeed there were amazing technical specialists, particularly in monasteries, who could recite by heart the most complicated prescribed combinations of hymns for various liturgical occasions, but were completely ignorant of all other aspects of liturgical singing. They were not interested, for example, in the origins of the Little Entrance at the Divine Liturgy, or why on Great and Holy Saturday at Matins the Gospel was read after the Great Doxology and not before the Kanon, as is usually the case. "Thus it is prescribed in the Typikon," was their only argument. Moreover, excursions into the history of the liturgy could have been looked upon as extreme latitudinarianism. Beyond a mere study of rubrics, liturgics at best consisted of a symbolic interpretation of liturgical actions, not based, however, on any definite historical or archeological facts.

Under these conditions and with such attitudes it is not surprising that church singing remained a purely practical subject. Each generation of church singers could only uncritically accept everything that was passed along by older generations, perhaps adding or deleting something according to personal tastes or opinions, and then pass the knowledge along to equally uncritical successive generations.

Here I must qualify my preceding remarks. It would be totally incorrect to assume that I am in any way downgrading the importance of practical knowledge and traditions in the area of liturgical singing (as I was accused of doing by some of the Russian listeners at my lectures). It is unquestionable that practical knowledge is essential; however, it must be founded upon theoretical knowledge as well, which includes liturgical musicology.

The first to recognize the importance of the history of liturgical singing in Russia was the prominent scholar and archeologist Metropolitan Evgenii (Bolkhovitinov) of Kiev (1767-1837; Metropolitan from 1822), while he was still an instructor at the theological seminary in Voronezh. However the first systematic, ground-laying works in the field of liturgical singing were undertaken only in the middle of the nineteenth century. The first such work was Церковное пение в России (Church singing in Russia; Moscow: 1867-9) by Rev. Dimitrii Razumovskii, whose contributions will be discussed in greater detail in following chapters. In this book, now quite obsolete, Razumovskii uncovered much information concerning liturgical singing that had been entirely unknown theretofore; at the same time his discoveries stimulated the interest of other researchers to explore the history and system of liturgical singing. Indeed it can be said that Razumovskii laid the foundations of Russian liturgical musicology.

Razumovskii's work was continued in many directions by such individuals as S. V. Smolenskii (1848-1909), Rev. V. M. Metallov (1862-1927), A. V. Preobrazhenskii (1870-1929), and Rev. I. I. Voznesenskii (1838-1918), to name only a few of the most prominent figures. As each new piece of research opened up new information and new problems requiring further examination, it became clear that the study of Russian Orthodox liturgical singing, of Russian liturgical musicology, was indeed a separate and worthy academic discipline and not merely an insignificant branch of general musicology or an exclusively practical subject.

The events of 1917 and the years following struck a catastrophic blow to the further development of both the art of liturgical singing and its scholarly investigation. At the same time it must be recognized that Soviet scholars find themselves in the most fruitful circumstances for continuing research in this field. We may assume that they have access to all of the manuscript repositories containing musical and liturgical monuments, as well as to archives containing vital documentary material. And in recent years it appears that research in the area of "music of the cult," as liturgical singing is now dubbed, has resumed, producing a small but steady trickle of publications. Among the Soviet researchers we must single out the theoretician and semeiographer M. V. Brazhnikov (now deceased) and the historian and liturgicist N. D. Uspenskii, Professor of the Leningrad Theological Academy.

The Appendix of this work contains a partially-annotated bibliography of the most important monographs and periodical literature dealing with Orthodox liturgical singing. A complete bibliography on the subject as well as a catalog of manuscripts and other primary sources, which would require an entire separate volume, is still a thing of the future.

CHAPTER I

The System of Orthodox Liturgical Singing: Concepts and Terminology

The Essence of Liturgical Singing

The differences in the structure of Orthodox sevices, as compared to the services of the Roman Catholic Church and, even more so, to those of various Protestant denominations, both determine and reflect divergent viewpoints concerning the significance of the musical element in worship, and hence, concerning the essence, forms and liturgical function of church music. Unless these differences are clearly identified from the start, one risks falling into various misconceptions which would ultimately lead to erroneous conclusions.

The first question that must be answered is: What is Orthodox liturgical singing in essence, and what role does it play in Orthodox worship?

Such a question may appear, at first glance, to be superfluous; the answer seems to be obvious without any further discussion necessary: Orthodox liturgical singing is vocal music—music produced by human voices alone—, which, in conjunction with words, accompanies worship services. This answer is understandable if one considers exclusively the choral singing found in the Russian Orthodox Church during approximately the last three centuries. Thus, one often hears mention, especially in non-Orthodox circles, of "Orthodox church *music*," to which all of the concepts concerning music in general can be applied. Even present-day Orthodox tend to view their liturgical singing simply as a category of vocal music (and a rather insignificant one even in that capacity), in which one can observe the same musical-aesthetic relationships found in secular music—the only such relationships recognized.

As a consequence of this viewpoint, singing at worship is often considered to be a *facultative* and non-essential element, instead of one that is *immanent* and inherent in worship. For this very same reason it remains unclear to many people why the Orthodox Church so categorically rejects any type of instrumental music in its services, even for the support of singing, to the extent that no instrument should even be permitted into the church, much less heard.

Ordinarily explanations for the ban on instrumental music are sought on the basis of ascetical tendencies, which are prominent in the Orthodox Church and in the Eastern churches in general. Indeed, such reasons are given by some Russian historians and theoreticians in the field of liturgical singing, who cite the views of certain Church Fathers upon this subject. These views are well-known: instrumental music was widely used by pagans at their religious ceremonies; Christians, on the other hand, should praise God not with inanimate artificial instruments, but with the most noble and natural instrument—the human voice.[1]

At this point it is not necessary to investigate further the justification for this point of view. The Slavic Orthodox churches merely adopted the principles of church singing, and therefore the non-acceptance of instrumental music in any form, from the Graeco-Byzantine Church, in which this viewpoint had already become firmly established. It is appropriate, however, to examine some other reasons for the non-admission of instrumental music into Orthodox services—reasons that lie in the very nature and form of Orthodox worship.

Orthodox worship consists almost exclusively of verbal expression in its many forms: prayer, glorification, instruction, exegesis, homily, etc. Only the word is capable of precisely expressing concrete, logically formulated ideas. Instrumental music, on the other hand, by its nature is incapable of such unambiguous expression; it can only express and evoke the emotional element, which is received subjectively by each individual listener, thus giving rise to a variety of interpretations. But it is impossible to give such an emotional reaction a precise, logical definition. Concepts such as sadness, majesty, joyfulness, happiness, etc. are merely general and vague characterizations of emotional qualities and do not represent any unequivocal ideas that can be precisely expressed in words. The same musical form, whether a simple tune played on a fife, a complex piece of instrumental polyphony, or even a melody hummed without words by the human voice, can be supplied with texts of different content and character that will enable the same music to convey completely diverse ideas. Only the word can give musical sounds a definite, unambiguous meaning. And in worship only the word can clearly express the ideas contained in prayer, instruction, contemplation, etc. Thus, wordless instrumental music by itself is not suited for conveying the concrete verbal content of worship. It can only entertain and please the ear, evoke various emotions, and, to a certain extent, reflect the emotional content of ideas expressed by words. On the other

---

[1] Dmitrii Razumovskii, Церковное пение в России [Church singing in Russia], Vol. 1 (Moscow: 1867), pp. 25-27; Vasilii Metallov, Очерк истории церковного пения в России [Essay on the history of church singing in Russia] (Moscow: n.p., 1900) pp. 37-38.

hand, the word taken in conjunction with musical sounds can combine logical clarity and precision of meaning with the emotional response to verbal ideas.

Herein, it seems, lies the reason why the musical element is admitted into the Orthodox liturgy only in conjunction with the word. Either the musical sounds give emotional coloration to the logically concrete contents of the liturgical texts, or the musical expression arises as an emotional reaction to the ideas expressed by the words.[2]

The emotional aspect of the musical element certainly has a good deal of significance in Orthodox worship, but in a manner different from churches that employ purely instrumental music in their services. If one takes the music by itself, devoid of words, one realizes that instrumental music can create only a certain mood or atmosphere, which can be characterized by the general terms mentioned above: sadness, majesty, joyfulness, etc. But these terms have no concrete ideas connected with them. Why is a piece of music sad or majestic? Only when the musical element becomes linked with the verbal is it possible to say why a given emotion arose as a result of the music and to explain by what concrete verbal ideas it was evoked.

In the case of unaccompanied singing the situation is entirely different. Here the emotional reaction is not brought about by a mood created by the music; rather, the mood first is created by reaction to the concrete ideas expressed in the text, and only then is it reflected by the character of the music, which is inseparably linked with the text. Despite the fact that canonical melodies (see Chapter III) remain constant in certain respects for a variety of texts, their emotional character coincides with the specific manner in which the nationality that originated those melodies perceives the ideas expressed by the corresponding texts.

Since Orthodox worship does not allow instrumental music in any form, but only musical sounds in conjunction with words, before

---

[2] Similar thoughts are expressed by the Benedictine scholar, Paolo Feretti, in his book, *Esthétique grégorienne*, (Paris: Desclée, 1938) p. 195: "Or la prière de l'Église n'est pas *individuelle*, j'allais dire égoiste, mais *objective, collective, sociale;* et de son coté, la musique qui l'accompagne, n'emprunte pas son expression à l'ordre purement émotif et sensuel, mais à un ordre supérieur, celui de l'intelligence. Sa subordination même la parte en quelque sorte à se cacher, et à prendre une expression, non point passionée, mais moderée et recuellie, objective et transcendentale." Furthermore, on p. 126 Feretti quotes Augusto Conti, *Il bello nel vero, o Estetica*, (Firenze: Le Monnier, 1891), cap. 59, Musica 5, 6, 7: "La musique a une relation indéfinie avec les sentiments, dans ce sens que les sons suscitant des sentiments discernables quant au genre et à l'espèce, mais non pas les particularités affectives, comme la parole peut faire."

one can speak about the concrete forms of liturgical singing it is necessary to discuss in general terms the musical element as it exists in the liturgy. In considering the most simple manifestations of the musical element one must include all aspects of the liturgy that are in any way connected with musical sounds: psalmody or recitation upon a single pitch, often described by the Latin term *recto tono,* as well as more elaborate styles of reading and exclamation, known as ekphonesis. Strictly speaking, these gradations of the musical element are not singing, but neither do they fall into the category of ordinary speech.

In fact, the ordinary conversational manner of speaking, as well as declamation, are not used in the Orthodox liturgy except in sermons.[3] Thus, every instance of congregational worship appears as a series of gradations of the musical phenomenon in intimate connection with the word. As the word is presented to the listener, there are no strict boundaries between these gradations: it is barely possible at times to distinguish singing from ekphonesis, ekphonesis from psalmody, etc. For this same reason it is hardly possible to consider singing proper merely as vocal music, apart from the liturgy.

Simple recitation *recto tono* on the one hand, and the luxuriant polyphonic singing of one or several large choirs on the other, are the two poles between which there exist many gradations, which are, nevertheless, quite closely connected with one another. One kind of musical setting flows out of another, determined by the content of the text and its position in the service. All of the different types and gradations of musical setting combine in the service to form an integrated musical whole in which the musical element serves to direct attention to the ideas expressed in the text and bring about an emotional reaction on the part of the listener.

There is not a single service, either public or private, in the Orthodox Church that does not contain singing either in the form of simple recitation or of a more complex nature. Moreover, in principle it makes no difference whether the singing is performed by a single singer, antiphonally by two highly-trained choirs, or by the entire congregation. In contrast to the Roman Catholic Church, the Orthodox Church has in its practice no such thing as a "low Mass," i.e. a service without singing. While there are parts of certain services, e.g. Compline or weekday Matins, that are not sung in the full sense of the word, they are still recited or "read" on a single note in the manner described above. Even private services, such as a Prayer Service

[3] In Greek and Serbian practice certain psalms and Old Testament readings are sometimes read in plain conversational speech.

(молебен) held in a private home, contain singing, often performed out of necessity by the officiating priest. The principle remains the same in all instances: the word is presented in an appropriate musical setting, in accordance with the character of the service and the logical content of the verbal text.

It becomes clear, then, that the liturgical singing of the Orthodox Church is one of the forms of worship itself. The Russians of past centuries referred to worship as "singing." "To go to sing" meant the same as "to go to worship." "It's time for singing, it's the hour for prayer! Lord Jesus Christ, our God, have mercy on us!"[4] With these words the monk on wake-up duty would rouse the brethren to Nocturn and Matins. The Stoglav Council of the Russian Orthodox Church in 1551 decreed that "... [the faithful] should come to the holy churches with [their] wives and children, and with faith and love should stand at all divine singing."[5] In the Typikon[6] all public worship services are designated as "singing": "It must be known that, as we have said earlier about singing, according to the tradition there is to be no other ordo in the cenobitic life than the one which requires the singing of particular psalms or some other service."[7]

It is apparent that if liturgical singing is indeed an aspect of worship, its forms should be determined by the forms of worship itself; in order to study the development of liturgico-musical forms, one must view them in conjunction with the evolution of the order of worship and in relation to the content of the liturgical texts.

Hymnography

The services of the Orthodox Church are extraordinarily rich in hymns[8] of varied content, which display a variety of textual and musical (i.e. liturgico-musical) forms. These hymns are inserted between prayers and readings, accompany processions of the clergy,

---

[4] "Пѣнію время, молитвѣ часъ. Господи Іисусе Христе Боже нашъ, помилуй насъ."

[5] Стоглав (Moscow: 1890) chap. 38, p. 160. See also pp. 161-162.

[6] *Translator's note:* In present usage, the word typikon (τὸ τυπικόν; типіконъ, уставъ) refers to that book which specifies how elements from the various cycles underlying Orthodox worship—annual, weekly, etc.—are to be combined in a given service.

[7] Типіконъ, сиесть уставъ (Moscow: Синодальная типографія, 1906) chap. 37, p. 45v.

[8] *Translator's note:* The term "hymn," an imperfect translation of the Russian term "песнопение," lit. "sung song," is used here to refer to any piece of liturgical song.

and are interwoven among psalm verses in an established order and in accordance with specific rules. The texts of the hymns are intended to focus the thoughts of the listener upon the central theme of a feast or upon the commemoration of a given saint. At other times, the hymns serve to instruct the congregation in the major dogmas of the Orthodox faith, often in a poetic, but nevertheless dogmatically pure form. Constituting a major portion of Orthodox services, the hymns contain the entire theological teaching of the Orthodox Church presented in a poetic, popular idiom suitable for singing. Thus it is sufficient for those attending the service merely to listen carefully to the hymns and the readings in order to receive the essential doctrines of the faith.[9] The musical element becomes the vehicle with the help of which the texts are more profoundly impressed upon the memory and consciousness of the listener and are, at the same time, interpreted emotionally.

The significance of the connection between the musical element and the text was emphasized by St. Basil the Great: "Inasmuch as the Holy Spirit knows that it is difficult to lead mankind toward virtue, that because of our inclination towards pleasure we are negligent of the path of righteousness, what does He do? To instruction He adds the pleasantness of sweet singing ($\mu\epsilon\lambda\omega\delta\iota\alpha$), so that together with what is delightful and harmonious to the ear we might receive in an imperceptible fashion that which is beneficial in the word. To this end the harmonious hymns of the psalms have been invented for us. . . ."[10]

These words are proven convincingly even in contemporary practice. Shortly before World War II in Orthodox and Uniate[11] village churches in the region known as Carpatho-Russia, singing at services was performed by the entire congregation. Each person had before him a book (сборник) containing all the prescribed hymns. An experienced cantor (дьяк) began the singing, and as

---

[9] The liturgical language employed in the various national branches of the Orthodox Church is, in most cases, an archaic form of a given nation's modern language. Thus, the Greek Church uses Middle Greek, a language used in the Byzantine Empire, while the Russian, Serbian and Bulgarian Orthodox, and Ukrainian Uniates employ Church Slavonic dating from the seventeenth century. Only certain groups, such as the Ukrainian Orthodox, use the modern form of the language. For the Slavic peoples, especially for the Russians, the difference between the liturgical and modern languages is not so great as to make the service incomprehensible. The difference lies not in the roots of the words, but in the grammatical forms. Thus the content of the hymns and the ideas contained therein remain understandable to the majority of the listeners.

[10] Migne, *Patrologia graeca* 32, col. 764; cited in Razumovskii, *op. cit.* p. 26.

soon as the familiar melody was heard, everyone—men, women and children—joined in the singing, performing the entire service in this manner. Even the children knew many of the texts by heart and could sing them from memory. In this way the musical element in the service played an important part in the religious education of the masses.[12]

Using as criteria the devotional and didactic aspects of liturgical singing it is possible to distinguish six different categories of hymns according to the character of their contents:

1. *Hymns in the strict sense of that word* (ὕμνοι, гимны) [13]: *poetic texts that offer to God praise (doxological hymns) or prayer (devotional hymns)*. An example is the hymn sung at the Divine Liturgy during the consecration of the Holy Gifts:

> We praise Thee,
> We bless Thee,
> We give thanks unto Thee, O Lord,
> And we pray unto Thee, O our God.

or the hymn sung at Great Vespers during the entrance of the clergy into the sanctuary through the Royal Doors:

> O gladsome light of the holy glory
> Of the immortal Father,
> Heavenly, holy, blessed Jesus Christ!
> Now that we have come to the setting of the sun
> And behold the light of evening,
> We praise God: Father, Son, and Holy Spirit.
> For meet it is at all times
> To worship Thee with voices of praise,

[11] *Translator's note:* The term "Uniate" refers here to groups of Orthodox particularly in the Western Ukraine who in the sixteenth-seventeenth centuries accepted the hierarchical leadership of the Roman Catholic papacy while at the same time maintaining Eastern liturgical rites.

[12] See Ivan A. Gardner, "Несколько соображений об общем пении за богослужением" [Several observations concerning congregational singing at services], Православная Русь (1969) No. 10; and "Еще об общем пении при богослужении" [More about congregational singing at services], *ibid.* (1969) No. 20.

[13] *Translator's note:* The hymn (ὕμνος; гимнъ) as a specific type of liturgical song is to be distinguished from the term used non-specifically (cf. n. 8 above).

O Son of God and Giver of Life.
Therefore all the world doth glorify Thee.

2. *Hymns of a dogmatic nature,* which express in poetic form certain key points of Orthodox doctrine, for example, the *theotokia-dogmatika* or *stichera dogmatika* (богородичны догматики) sung at Saturday evening Vespers at the end of the verses following "Lord, I call upon Thee." The dogmatika relate the dogmas of the incarnation of Christ and the virginity of the Mother of God. The example given below is the Theotokion-Dogmatikon of the Fifth Tone:

In the Red Sea of old
A type of the virgin bride was prefigured.
There Moses divided the waters.
Here Gabriel assisted in the miracle.
There Israel crossed the sea without getting wet.
Here the Virgin gave birth to Christ without seed.
After Israel's passage, the sea remained impassible.
After Emmanuel's birth, the Virgin remained a virgin.
O ever-existing God, who appeared as man:
O Lord, have mercy on us!

3. *Hymns that describe historical events.* An example is the sticheron (see p. 36) on the Litiia [14] of the Nativity of Christ (in the fifth tone):

The Magi, Kings of Persia, knew with assurance
That Thou, the Heavenly King, wast born on earth;
Led by the light of a star they came to Bethlehem
And offered their chosen gifts,
Gold, frankincense and myrrh.
Falling before Thee they worshipped Thee,
For they saw Thee who art timeless,
Lying as a babe in the cave.

4. *Hymns of a moralistic nature,* which contain no prayer to God, but speak directly to the listener in the manner of a sung sermon. An example is a verse from the stichera aposticha (see pp. 35-36) sung at Vespers of the first Monday of Great Lent (in the third tone):

[14] The Litiia is inserted into feast-day Vespers and consists of a series of petitions recited by the clergy in the narthex.

Let us keep a worthy fast,
One acceptable to the Lord.
A true fast is the shunning of evil,
Control of the tongue, estrangement from anger,
The setting aside of all sensuality, gossip,
falsehood and swearing.
The weakening of all these will make the fast
true and well-pleasing.

5. *Hymns of a contemplative nature.* An example is the sticheron on the Praises (see p. 36) sung on Great and Holy Saturday (in the second tone):

Today the grave holds Him who holds creation
in the palm of His hand.
A stone covers Him who covers the heavens
with virtue.
Life sleeps and Hell trembles,
And Adam is set free from his bonds.
Glory to Thy dispensation!
Through it Thou hast fulfilled all the eternal
Sabbath rest
And hast granted us Thy most holy Resurrection
from the dead.

6. *Hymns that accompany liturgical actions, relating in poetic form the symbolic meaning contained in those actions.* These hymns are very few in number, and are addressed to the listener in most cases. An example is the Cherubic Hymn, during the singing of which the bread and wine to be used in the Eucharist are carried from the Table of Preparation to the Altar in solemn procession. The character of this hymn is mixed, combining both the contemplative element and an explanation of the symbolism contained in the liturgical action:

Let us who mystically represent the cherubim
And who sing the thrice-holy hymn
To the life-creating Trinity,
Now lay aside all earthly cares,
That we may receive the King of all,
Who comes invisibly upborne
By the angelic hosts. Alleluia.

From these few representative examples it can be seen how

liturgical texts play an important role in the fundamental theological education of the worshipper, especially when the entire congregation participates in singing them.

Two extremely important factors that shape liturgical singing are the order of services and the various sacred rites and ceremonial actions that take place during worship. Many hymns, particularly those of the Divine Liturgy, are sung during "quiet" or "secret" prayers—prayers that are read softly by the celebrant and are then interrupted by audible exclamations, forming an integrated whole with the hymns. Other hymns are performed during processions of the clergy around the church or during the censing of the church's interior by the deacon or priest. Parts of certain services are performed either in the middle of the church or in the narthex (e.g. the Litiia). Thus, the hymns that are specified to be sung during these actions or that serve to fill the time between actions must correspond in duration to the actions or prayers that they accompany. This, in turn, affects the musical organization of the service, since the Orthodox Church does not permit gaps in the ritual to be filled with instrumental music.

In the system of Orthodox services, the greatest didactic significance is found in Vespers and Matins. (In the Russian Orthodox Church it is common practice to combine these two services on certain occasions into one liturgical unit known as the All-Night Vigil [всенощное бдение].) The Vespers and Matins services are particularly rich in changing hymnographical material. Into the unchanging framework of these two services, which consists to a great extent of psalms, is inserted a wealth of didactic and devotional material in the form of hymns of varying content. This material, which is constantly changing depending on the day of the week, the number of the week in the year, the day of the month, and the prevailing tone, conveys the central liturgical theme of the given day, and guides the mind of the listener in the appropriate direction. In this central theme is contained the ideological content of the given day and the given service. By contrast, the Divine Liturgy contains little such didactic material, and then only in the first part, the "Liturgy of the Catechumens." The main part, the "Liturgy of the Faithful," is quite constant in its makeup and consists almost entirely of devotional hymns. Thus the richest variety of the musical element in Orthodox worship is displayed primarily in the musical organization of Vespers and Matins, in the form of varying tones, different types of melodies belonging to a given tone and varying styles of performance.

Styles of Performance

The structure of the service and the liturgical functions of the musically presented texts determine the manner in which these texts are performed. The styles of performance are in principle identical in all the national branches of the Orthodox Church, and some of them are found also in the Western Church, which points to their ancient origin. The musical forms that arise out of the different styles of performance determine the musical format of the service, each having a specific place in the service prescribed and regulated by the Typikon. While there may be some deviations from the norm in different regions or periods of history, the principle remains unchanged.

The styles of musical performance of liturgical texts can be divided into two categories:

1. Performance by a soloist—a celebrant, reader or cantor. This category includes psalmody (or recitation) and ekphonesis, which by definition cannot be executed by more than one performer. (Not included in this category is execution by a single performer out of necessity, when performance by a choir is specified.)

2. Performance by a choir—a group of singers of an unspecified number—in unison or polyphonically.

Ekphonesis and psalmody may, in turn, be divided into three distinct styles:

1. The exclamation of short prayers or petitions, consisting usually of one or a very few short phrases or sentences. Included in this category are petitions of litanies and closing doxologies pronounced by the priest at the end of litanies.

2. A more chant-like recitation of certain prayers that borders between psalmody and ekphonesis.

3. Solemn reading employed in the delivery of the Holy Scripture, known in the Western Church as *lectio solemnis*.

The choral mode of performance may also be divided into five distinct styles, each of which is prescribed in specific instances by the Typikon:

1. *Antiphonal style.* In principle, this style involves two choirs

stationed at the right and left of the Icon Screen (*ikonostasis*). Both choirs, the right and the left, sing in alternation: first, the right choir sings a hymn or verse in its entirety, then the left choir sings the next hymn, also in its entirety. This style is employed primarily for the performance of stichera and psalms that are performed verse by verse. Similarly, in the case of lengthy hymns, such as the Great Doxology, the hymn is divided into sections that are alternately performed by the right and left choirs.[15]

2. *Epiphonal and hypophonal style.* The first term refers to the procedure of prefacing each verse of a psalm with a certain unchanging verse. Thus, an epiphon is a refrain that precedes the verse. By contrast, a hypophon is an unchanging refrain that follows a psalm verse. This style can have two variations: (a) The choir sings the constant refrain to verses which are psalmodized by a single reader; this may be done by only the right or left choir or by both in alternation. (b) Both the refrain and the verse are sung chorally, either by a single choir or by both choirs in alternation.

3. *Responsorial style.* This style also includes two variations: (a) The choir responds by repeatedly singing a given text after each petition or exclamation of the celebrant. In such instances only one choir, the right or the left, or the entire congregation sings. A good example of this variety of responsorial singing can be found in litanies, where each petition intoned by the celebrant is followed by the sung response "Lord, have mercy" or "Grant it, O Lord." (b) The reader reads a series of verses from a given psalm, while the choir responds by singing the first verse intoned by the reader. This response is sung alternately by both choirs. In closing, the reader intones the first half of the initial verse, while the singers respond with the second half of the verse. An example of the second variety of responsorial style is found in the performance of prokeimena (see p. 49).

4. *Canonarchal style.* This style, particularly widespread in Russian monasteries, is almost a distinguishing feature of monastic singing. In many respects it resembles responsorial style and can easily be confused with the latter. In essence, however, canonarchal style is quite different. It can be best described as "singing with a prompter," since the function of the canonarch is similar to that of

[15] The principle of double-choir singing (antiphonal singing) has all but disappeared from contemporary liturgical practice. As a rule the singing is now performed by a single choir. But prior to 1917 many parishes in Moscow and other Russian cities still practiced antiphonal singing. In Greek practice even today, however, if there are only two singers present, one will take his place on the right of the church and the other on the left in order to sing antiphonally.

the prompter in the theater.[16] The canonarch intones the text of a hymn, phrase after phrase, on a single pitch, while the choir repeats each phrase in a more elaborate musical setting. This procedure allows a large number of singers to sing without a book in front of them; only the canonarch needs the book, which he uses to prompt the rest of the singers. This style of singing is used primarily for constantly changing hymns (propers), such as stichera.

With very few exceptions, canonarchal style is not used in cathedrals and parish churches, since all of the singing there is performed by trained choirs. But in situations where congregational singing is practiced, singing with a canonarch acquires great practical significance.

5. *Hymn style.* In this style the choir sings a given hymn from beginning to end without interruption. In this manner are performed, for example, the Cherubic Hymn of the Divine Liturgy, and the greater part of the hymns from the Liturgy of the Faithful, unchanging (ordinary) hymns from Vespers and Matins, such as "O Gladsome Light," and occasionally, certain propers of major feasts. Also performed in this manner are hymns that are sung during certain ceremonial actions; examples of such hymns are the theotokia-dogmatika, during which the clergy moves in procession into the sanctuary through the Royal Doors, or the hymns sung during the vesting of the bishop in the middle of the church before the beginning of Divine Liturgy.

All the different modes and styles of performance discussed above have been precisely regulated by various liturgical books from the earliest times to this day. It should be noted, however, that over the centuries certain rules cited in the most ancient typika underwent changes as liturgico-musical traditions changed. Certain styles of performance changed their position in the liturgy or became applicable to different cycles or types of hymns. Certain hymns with time lost their initial significance, either as a result of specific liturgical reforms or in the course of centuries of evolution. This was the case, for example, with the gradual replacement of the "choral office" (ἀσματικὴ ἀκολουθία; песенное последование) [17] and the Typi-

---

[16] Cf. the discussion of Jacobus Goar in his *Euchologion sive rituale Graecorum* (Venice, 1730; reprint ed., Graz: Akademische Druck- und Verlagsanstalt, 1960), p. 26.

[17] See M. Lisitsyn, Первоначальный славяно-русский типикон [The first Slavic-Russian Typikon], (St. Petersburg: 1911) p. 24 et passim; Vasilii Metallov, Богослужебное пение русской церкви в период домонгольский [The liturgical singing of the Russian Church in the pre-Mongol period], (Moscow: 1912).

kon of the Monastery of the Studios by the Jerusalem Typikon, which is employed in its essential aspects to this day by monastery, cathedral and parish churches alike. New hymns and styles of performance supplanted older ones; new ways of grouping hymns in the service developed; textual, melodic and tonal forms changed, as did the very musical organization of certain services. The principle behind musical performance in the liturgy, however, remained unchanged.

Types of Hymns

In the course of the discussions to follow it will be necessary to deal with the names of various hymns. Although this may lie more properly in the area of liturgics and Byzantine liturgical poetry, it seems advisable at this point to identify and define the various types of hymns and their basic forms.[18] The name of a given hymn depends to a great extent upon the position it occupies in the scheme of a particular service and upon the overall musical format of the service. The textual and musical organization of a service result in a type of "tension curve" to which individual hymns can be related.

The names of hymns refer to several aspects:

1. The poetic and musical form of the liturgical text.
2. The position of the given hymn in the fixed, unchanging scheme of a particular service.
3. The mode of performance of the given hymn.
4. The position of the singers and/or the congregation during the performance of the hymn.

With regard to the types and names of the hymns themselves there are no absolutely clear boundaries that separate one type from another. It is possible for a single hymn with the same text to be identified in two different ways, depending on the place it occupies in the scheme of a given service. For example, the same text may be called a *troparion* in one instance, a *sedalen* in another, and an *antiphon* in a third; and, as a result of such redesignation, its musical form may either change or remain the same. Almost all names of hymns in Orthodox terminology are taken from the Greek. They

---

[18] See also Lazar Mirkovic, Православна литургика или наука о богослужењу православне источне цркве [Orthodox liturgics or the study of the liturgy of the Orthodox Church], Vol. 1, (1919; reprint ed., Belgrade, 1965) pp. 219-239.

are given below in their anglicized form, followed by the original Greek and the Church Slavonic.

1. *Sticheron* (pl. *stichera*) (τὸ στιχερόν, τὰ στιχηρά; стихира, стихиры). Stichera are poetic verses of varying content and length, having usually between 8 and 12 lines, set to a corresponding number of melodic lines. In performance a group of stichera is commonly inserted between the verses of a psalm in such a way that the psalm verse precedes the sticheron; less often, the psalm verse follows the sticheron. In performance by two choirs each sticheron of a group is performed by only one of the choirs, often with a canonarch. If, however, the Typikon calls for a given sticheron to be repeated, it is repeated by the opposite choir. When a canonarch is involved, the psalm verses preceding the sticheron are performed responsorially: the canonarch intones the first half of the verse, while the choir answers by singing the second half. In Church Slavonic terminology the preceding psalm verses are termed *zapev* (запѣвъ; pl. запѣвы), meaning "introductory intonation." Thus, if the tone of the next sticheron is different from the one preceding, the canonarch announces the change before the *zapev*, then sings the *zapev* in the new tone, thus literally giving the intonation for the sticheron to follow.

Stichera fall into the following categories:

A. *Stichera on "Lord, I call upon Thee"* (στιχηρὰ εἰς τὸ Κύριε ἐκέκραξα; стихиры на господи воззвахъ): Vespers stichera that are woven into the Vespers Psalms 140 (141), 141 (142), 129 (130), and 116 (117).[19] On particularly festive occasions when the Typikon prescribes ten stichera on "Lord, I call upon Thee," these stichera are interpolated after verse 8 of Psalm 141; if only eight stichera are indicated, the interpolation occurs after verse 1 of Psalm 129.[20] At daily Vespers, when only six stichera are called for, the interpolation begins after verse 3 of Psalm 129. Finally, for the service of Little Vespers, which is now served only in a few monasteries, only four stichera are required, and they are included after verse 5 of Psalm 116.

B. The *stichera aposticha* (στιχηρὰ ἀπὸ στίχους, στιχηρὰ εἰς τὰ στίχον; стихиры стиховны, стихиры на стиховнѣхъ). This

---

[19] *Translator's note:* The numbers in parentheses indicate the numbering of the Psalms according to the Hebrew Bible, which is employed by most Protestant churches. The Eastern Orthodox Church uses the Septuagint (Greek) numbering for the Psalms, which is also employed by the Roman Catholic Church. Hereafter only the Septuagint numbers will be given.

[20] When an entrance of the clergy through the Royal Doors into the Sanctuary is specified during Vespers, it takes place during the singing of the last sticheron of this group. Also, if there are two choirs, the last four stichera of this group are sung by both choirs joined together in the center of the church.

group of stichera is performed in the second half of Vespers, after the entrance. Normally only four stichera are prescribed. The difference between the stichera aposticha and the stichera on "Lord, I call upon Thee" is that in the case of the former the psalm verse follows, rather than precedes each sticheron. Moreover, while the psalm verses employed in conjunction with Group A are unchanging, the psalm verses for Group B change according to the day of the week and the occasion being celebrated. There is also a group of stichera aposticha for weekday Matins, which are interpolated into verses 15-17 of Psalm 89.

C. *Stichera on the Praises* (στιχηρὰ εἰς τοὺς Αἴνους; стихиры на хвалитехъ).[21] This group of stichera is found only in Sunday or feast-day Matins, and is inserted into the unit formed by Psalms 148, 149, and 150. When six stichera are prescribed, they are included after verse 9 of Psalm 149; when only four stichera are designated, the inclusion begins after verse 2 of Psalm 150.

D. *Stichera on the Litiia* (στιχηρὰ εἰς τὴν λιτήν; стихиры на литіи). The stichera of this group are sung without any psalm verses during the Litiia, which occurs during feast-day Vespers. The singing of the stichera accompanies the exit of the clergy into the narthex, or, in some monasteries, a procession around the church.

E. *Stichera on the Beatitudes* (μακαρισμοί; стихиры блаженны). This special group of stichera is sung only at Divine Liturgy on Sundays, interpolated into the verses of the Sermon on the Mount (Matt. 5:3-12) that usually constitute the Third Antiphon. Altogether there are nine stichera for each of the eight tones.

In all of the stichera groups discussed above, the last sticheron is preceded by the Lesser Doxology: "Glory to the Father and to the Son and to the Holy Spirit, both now and ever and unto ages of ages, amen." This doxology is indicated in liturgical books by the abbreviation "Glory: both now and ever" (Δόξα καὶ νῦν; слава и нынѣ). But occasionally the Lesser Doxology is divided in half: after "Glory . . ." follows the penultimate sticheron, then "both now and ever . . ." and the final sticheron, which usually deals with the Mother of God. In this case only the abbreviation "Glory . . ." (Δόξα; слава) appears before the penultimate sticheron, and "both now and ever" (καὶ νῦν; и нынѣ) before the final one.

F. There exist also individual stichera that either stand alone in a given service or follow single psalms not included in any psalm

---

[21] The Greeks also term this group "πασαπνοάρια" from the initial words: "Let everything that breathes . . ." (" Πᾶσα πνοὴ αἰνεσάτο τὸν Κύριον").

cycle. Such stichera, for example, are found in festal Matins following Psalm 50. Other stichera in this category derive their names from the content of their text and are reserved for special occasions: *theotokion-dogmatikon* (θεοτοκίον δογματικόν; богородиченъ догматикъ), an example of which is found on p. 28; *anastasimon* (ἀναστάσιμον; воскресенъ), a sticheron in praise of the Resurrection; *theotokion* (θεοτόκιον; богородиченъ), a sticheron in praise of the Mother of God; *stavrotheotokion* (σταυροθεοτόκιον; кресто-богородиченъ), a sticheron commemorating the suffering of the Mother of God at the Cross; *stavroanastasimon* (σταυροαναστά-σιμον; крестовоскресенъ), commemorating the Cross and the Resurrection; *martyrikon* (μαρτυρικόν; мученыченъ), sung in praise of one or several martyrs; *triadikon* (τριαδικόν; троиченъ), in praise of the Holy Trinity; *nekrosima* (νεκρώσιμα; мертвенна or покой-на), in praise of the departed.

G. Finally, there is one more important group of eleven stichera, the Matins *Gospel Stichera* (στιχηρὰ ἑωθινά; стихиры евангель-скія), which are related in content to the eleven Resurrection Gospel readings read at Sunday Matins. These stichera, together with the Gospel readings, form an eleven-week cycle that is repeated throughout the year. Each sticheron is sung to one of the eight tones, the first eight to tones 1-8, and numbers 9, 10, and 11, to tones 5, 6, and 8, respectively. In the course of ordinary Sunday Matins these stichera are sung as part of the stichera on the Praises, after "Glory." In liturgical chant-books these eleven stichera are supplied with particularly rich and florid melodies.

Stichera as a whole are extremely important from a hymnographical and liturgical standpoint. They communicate the main theme of a given day—an event from the New Testament or the life of a saint. They are the hymns that serve the most to direct the thoughts of the worshippers in a particular direction. Sung, for the most part, to relatively simple melodies of a syllabic or neumatic character with only an occasional melismatic passage, stichera display a tight connection between the music and the text, and thus are more easily memorized by the listener. The last sticheron in a particular group, sometimes called the *doxastikon* (δοξαστικόν; славникъ) since it is sung after the doxology, on Great Feasts to a more florid melody than on lesser feasts or ordinary days.[22]

[22] Stichera were originally collected separately in a book called the Sticherarion (Στιχηράριον; стихирарь). With time, however, the stichera for various occasions were regrouped according to the order of service and included alongside other hymns (troparia, kanons, etc.) in other liturgical books, such as the Oktoechos, Menaion, and Triodion.

2. *Troparion* (τὸ τροπάριον; тропарь). A troparion is a stanza
in which the central liturgical theme of a given day or service is summarized.[23] An example is the troparion for the Nativity of Christ (in
the fourth tone):

> Thy Nativity, O Christ our God,
> Has shone to the world the light of wisdom;
> For by it those who worshipped the stars
> Were taught by a star to adore Thee,
> The Sun of Righteousness,
> And to know Thee, the Orient from on high.
> O Lord, glory to Thee!

or the troparion for Easter (in the fifth tone):

> Christ is risen from the dead,
> Trampling down death by death,
> And upon those in the tombs
> Bestowing life.

The troparion is sung or recited *recto tono* at various services of
the given day and is often repeated a number of times during the same
service. At Vespers it is sung towards the end of the service, before
the dismissal; at Matins—at the beginning and at the end, after the
Great Doxology; at Divine Liturgy—after the Little Entrance and
also, on Great Feasts of the Lord,[24] interpolated into the psalm verses
that constitute the festal Third Antiphon. In contrast to stichera,
where each psalm verse is followed by a different sticheron, in the
Third Antiphon of Liturgy the same troparion is repeated after each
psalm verse.

In some cases, however, the same psalm verse is repeated a
number of times while the troparia change. Thus, for example, in
Sunday Matins and in the Matins for the departed, following the
reading of Psalm 118, a cycle of five troparia is sung, preceded each
time by verse 12 of the aforementioned psalm.[25]

[23] Goar, *op. cit.* p. 26, gives the following definition for a troparion:
"τροπάριον. Vox generica est, et cunctis canticis in Ecclesia Graeca receptis,
communis: Modulum ubique interpretamur: et alibi rationem reddimus Quoad
sui compositionem Latinis Antiphonis similis est, quamvis Antiphonam ulla
ratione interpretari, nequeamus."

[24] I.e., the Nativity of Christ, the Theophany, Palm Sunday, Easter, the
Ascension, Pentecost, the Transfiguration, and the Elevation of the Holy Cross.

[25] Also known as Ἄμωμοι; непорочны; Latin: *Beati immaculati.* The

On occasion, a group of stanzas that are designated in liturgical books as troparia are sung consecutively, without intervening psalm verses (as are the stichera in group D above). An example of this is found during the procession to the Blessing of the Water on the Feast of Theophany or during a Lesser Blessing of the Water. In this case the distinction between troparia and stichera becomes clouded; such troparia take on the character of stichera. (An exceptional case is presented by the groups of troparia found within the odes of a kanon. This exception will be discussed below.)

The same hymn that in one instance is designated as a troparion may, as the result of a different context and placement in the service, be designated by another name. Thus, for example, the troparion for the Sunday of St. Thomas,[26] "From the sealed tomb Thou didst shine forth" (in tone 7), is designated as a *sedalen* after the second kathisma [27] for every Sunday Matins in the seventh tone; but in other instances the sedalen is designated as a troparion.[28] In the first case the name of the hymn is determined by the manner in which it is performed, while in the second case, the name is derived from its placement in the scheme of the service and the position of the congregation during its performance. Thus it is possible to define a sedalen as a troparion sung in certain designated places in the service (following a kathisma of the Psalter and after the third ode of a kanon) during the singing of which the congregation is permitted to sit.

The content of a troparion can take on the same characteristics as special stichera (of Group F), i.e. theotokion, stavrotheotokion, martyrikon, etc., with the exception of a dogmatikon.

The troparion of the day sung at the close of Vespers is termed an *apolytikion* (ἀπολυτίκιον; отпустителенъ) or dismissal troparion, since it directly precedes the dismissal. If several events or saints are commemorated on the same day, it is possible to combine several troparia in the same service.

Greeks also call these troparia εὐλογητάρια, from the twelfth verse of Psalm 118, which begins: "εὐλογητὸς εἶ Κύριε..."

[26] The first Sunday after Easter.

[27] *Translator's note:* In Greek the "sedalen" is called a "kathisma" (κάθισμα). However, in Slavonic liturgical terminology the term "kathisma" (кафизма) has a different meaning, referring to the twenty divisions of the Psalter. In Greek these twenty divisions are called στιχολογία. Since this work deals primarily with Slavic liturgical practice, the Slavonic terminology will be employed hereafter for these two terms.

[28] E.g., in the *Contacarium Mosquense*, (Copenhagen: Monumenta Musicae Byzantinae, 1960), p. 168v., a hymn is called a troparion, while the present-day Menaion terms the same hymn a sedalen after the second kathisma at Matins for the fourteenth of September.

The musical setting of troparion texts is most commonly syllabic.[29]

3. *Kanon* (ὁ κανών; канонъ). A kanon is an extended poem consisting of nine odes (ᾠδή, пѣснь; pl. ᾠδαί, пѣсни), which are based, respectively, on nine Biblical canticles:

The first, on Exodus 15: 1-19 and 21,
The second, on Deuteronomy 32: 1-43,
The third, on I Samuel 2: 1-10,
The fourth, on Habakkuk 3: 1-19,
The fifth, on Isaiah 26: 9-19,
The sixth, on Jonah 2: 1-9,
The seventh, on Daniel 3: 26-51a,
The eighth, on Daniel 3: 51b-88,
The ninth, in praise of the Mother of God,
                                     on Luke 1:46-55 or 63-79.

Each ode of the kanon consists of an initial stanza, the *heirmos* (εἱρμός; ирмосъ or "связка"), lit., "link," and a set of two, three, or occasionally more troparia-stanzas, which in meter, number of syllables (in the Greek original) and melody are identical to the heirmos. By its content the heirmos serves as a connecting link between the theme of the Old Testament canticles and the New Testament theme that is developed in the troparia of the given ode. An illustrative example of the metrical relationship between a Greek heirmos and its troparia can be seen in the first ode of the second kanon for Pentecost [30] (in the seventh tone):

Heirmos [31]

1. Πόντῳ	2 syllables
2. Ἐκάλυψε φαραὼ σὺν ἄρμασιν	11 syllables
3. Ὁ συνίβων πολέμους	7 syllables
4. Ἐν ὑψηλῷ βραχίονι	7(8) syllables
5. Ἄσωμεν αὐτῷ	5 syllables
6. Ὅτι δεδόξασται.	6 syllables

[29] In ancient Russian practice the troparion was recited and only its last phrase was sung. For this reason only these final phrases are supplied with musical notation in ancient Russian liturgical singing-books.

[30] Composed by Kosmas, Bishop of Maium, in the eight century.

[31] *Pentecostarion* (Rome: 1883), p. 396. The melodic phrases, which are not notated with neumes, are marked with asterisks in this edition.

Troparion 1

1. "Εργῳ	2 syllables
2. Ὡς πάλαι τοῖς Μαθηταῖς ἐπηγγείλω	11 syllables
3. Τὸ Παράκλητον Πνεῦμα	7 syllables
4. Ἐξαποστείλας Χριστὲ	7 syllables
5. "Ελαμψας τὸ φῶς	5 syllables
6. Κόσμῳ φιλάνθρωπε.	6 syllables

Troparion 2

1. Νόμῳ	2 syllables
2. Τὸ πάλαι προκηρυχθὲν καὶ προφήταις	11 syllables
3. Ἐπληρώθη· τοῦ θείου	7 syllables
4. Πνεύματος σήμερον	6 syllables
5. Πᾶσι γὰρ πιστοῖς	5 syllables
6. Χάρις ἐκκέχυται.	6 syllables

As can be seen from this example, each troparion of the ode has almost the exact number of syllables—2, 11, 7, 7(8), 7(6), 5, 6—per line as the heirmos and an almost identical pattern of accents. The melody of the heirmos, therefore, is easily transferable to the troparia. However, in translation to Church Slavonic or another language this congruence between the heirmos and troparia is lost: the number of syllables and, particularly, the accentuation pattern are inevitably destroyed, as can be seen from the example below:[32]

[32] The thirteenth-century Greek MS, Codex Coislin 220, p. 182r., found in the Bibliothèque Nationale of Paris, and the Novgorod Heirmologion (see Erwin Koschmieder, *Die altesten Novgoroder Hirmologien-Fragmente*, I, [Munich: 1952], p. 218) of the same period give a different division of the melodic phrases:

1. Πόντῳ ἐκάλυψε	6 syllables
2. Φαραὼ σὺν ἅρμασιν	7 syllables
3. Ὁ συντρίβων πολέμους	7 syllables
4. Τῇ κραταιᾷ δυνάμει Χριστὸς	9 syllables
5. "Ασωμεν αὐτῷ ὅτι δεδόξασται.	11 syllables

1. Въ понте покры	5 syllables
2. Фараопа со оружиїемъ	10 syllables
3. Съкрушаїаи брани	7 syllables
4. Высокою мышцею	8 syllables
5. Поимъ їемоу їако прославися	11 syllables

It must be remembered that in the Slavonic text the half-vowels "ъ" and "ь" were at that time syllable-forming and were supplied with neumatic signs.

Heirmos

1. Понтомъ	2 syllables
2. Покры фараона съ колесницами	11 syllables
3. Сокрушаяй брани	6 syllables
4. Мышцею высокою	7 syllables
5. Поимъ ему	4 syllables
6. Яко прославися	6 syllables

Troparion 1

1. Деломъ	2 syllables
2. Якоже древле ученикомъ обещал еси	14 syllables
3. Утешителя духа	7 syllables
4. Пославый Христе	5(6) syllables
5. Возсіялъ еси міру	7 syllables
6. Свѣтъ человѣколюбче	7 syllables

Troparion 2

1. Закономъ	3 syllables
2. Древле проповѣданное и пророки	12 syllables
3. Исполнися: божественнаго бо	10 syllables
4. Духа днесь	3 syllables
5. Всѣмъ вѣрнымъ	3 syllables
6. Благодать излияся	7 syllables

There is divergence not only in the number of syllables and the pattern of accentuation between the Greek original and the Church Slavonic translation, but also between the heirmos and its corresponding troparia.

The second ode of the kanon is commonly omitted in present-day practice due to the severe and gloomy character of the second Biblical canticle (from Deuteronomy) upon which it is based. Thus, today the kanon consists of only eight odes, with the exception of the kanons for the next-to-the-last Saturday of Great Lent and the seventh Saturday after Easter (the Saturday before Pentecost), which have preserved their second odes. Both of these days commemorate the departed. Also, the Great Penitential Kanon of St. Andrew of Crete has a second ode.

In addition to complete kanons (with or without the second ode) there are partial kanons found in the services before the Nativity and Theophany and those of Great Lent. Thus, a *diodion* (διώδιον;

двупѣснецъ) consists of only two odes, the eighth and the ninth, while a *triodion* (τριώδιον; трипѣснецъ) consists of three odes; in the case of the latter, the eighth and ninth odes remain constant, while the remaining ode changes with each day of the week: the first ode is sung on Monday, the second on Tuesday, the third on Wednesday, the fourth on Thursday, the fifth on Friday, and sixth and seventh on Saturday, forming, together with the eighth and ninth, a *tetraodion* (τετραώδιον; четверопѣснецъ). These partial kanons are combined on a given day with the complete kanons dedicated to the saint(s) of the day. Each kanon, whether complete or partial, can be set in a tone that is different from that of the other kanons with which it is combined. For this reason there occurs a constant modulation from one tone to another in this part of the Matins service, resulting in a considerable degree of musical variety.

The kanon, which occupies a central position in Matins, is divided into three sections separated one from another by Little Litanies and other short hymns—sedalens, hypakoe, and kontakia with oikos. The odes are grouped as follows: (a) 1, (2), 3; (b) 4, 5, 6; and (c) 7, 8, 9. The ninth ode is usually preceded by the singing of the Magnificat ("My soul magnifies the Lord . . ." Luke 1:46-55) with the refrain "More honorable than the Cherubim. . .," while on Great Feasts special refrains to the Mother of God replace the Magnificat. Depending on the rank of the feast, each ode of the kanon or each group of odes is ended by an heirmos from the last ode in the group; this heirmos, however, is usually taken from a kanon other than those comprising the kanon group of the given day. When circumstances allow, this final heirmos is sung by both the right and left choirs combined in the center of the church (see Katabasia, p. 51).[33]

In accordance with the event or saint being commemorated on a given day, it is possible to have several kanons combined during a single Matins service. For example, on a given Sunday it is possible to have the following combination: a resurrectional kanon of a given tone combined with a kanon to the Mother of God as well as one or even two kanons in honor of saints. In this instance, the first odes of each kanon are performed in order, followed by the subsequent odes. The rules for combining kanons during week-days of Great Lent are especially complicated.

Based on existing evidence from ancient liturgical books, originally both the heirmos and troparia of a given ode were sung in alternation with verses from the corresponding Old Testament canticle. This practice is still followed occasionally during Great Lent.

[33] See the Typikon, chap. 19, p. 33.

But generally in present-day practice the Old Testament canticles are omitted entirely; each troparion is preceded instead by a refrain— an epiphon— pertaining to the feast or saint being commemorated, e.g., "Glory to Thee, our God, glory to Thee," "O most blessed Father Nicholas, pray unto God for us," etc. The penultimate troparion is preceded by "Glory..." while the last one by "both now and ever...." It is also present-day practice to sing only the heirmos of each ode, while the troparia are recited *recto tono*. The entire kanon, including the heirmos and the troparia, is sung only on Easter.[34]

All heirmoi are collected in a liturgical chantbook known as the *Heirmologion* (Είρμολόγιον; Ирмологий). It is noteworthy that the arrangement of the heirmoi in ancient Greek heirmologia is somewhat different than in Russian manuscripts of the same period. In the Greek heirmologia of the twelfth and thirteenth centuries the heirmoi of a single kanon are arranged one after another in order of the odes; moreover, the kanons are grouped according to the eight tones. In ancient Russian heirmologia the heirmoi are also grouped according to the eight tones, but the heirmoi of every kanon of a given tone are grouped by ode. Thus, for each tone, there first appear all heirmoi of the first ode, then the heirmoi of the second ode, etc.[35]

The basis for this difference in the arrangement of heirmoi between the Greek and Russian churches must still be thoroughly examined. The solution to this question may shed further light on the investigation of whether ancient Russian singing of the eleventh and twelfth centuries was merely Byzantine singing exactly transplanted onto Russian soil, or whether Russian liturgical singing displayed independent traits from the most ancient times.

The melodies of the heirmoi are all of a syllabic character.

---

[34] In present-day practice the Greeks still sing not only the heirmoi but also all the troparia of kanons. The Russians, on the other hand, sing only the heirmoi, while the troparia are read. The entire kanon (heirmoi and troparia) is sung only on Easter in present-day Russian practice. As late as the seventeenth century the entire kanon for Palm Sunday was was also sung. There is evidence that various kanons were occasionally sung in their entirety during the reign of Peter the Great (reigned 1696-1725). In ancient Russia it was the practice to sing entire kanons, and some ancient Russian liturgical singing-books contain neumatic notation not only for the heirmoi, but also for the troparia (see, e.g., *Fragmenta Chiliandarica, A. Sticherarium* [Copenhagen: Monumenta Musicae Byzantinae, 1957], pp. 51r-53v). However, the Stoglav Council of 1551 decreed in its Rule 1 that kanons must be recited instead of sung.

[35] See E. Koschmieder, *op. cit.* Vol. II, (Munich, 1955), pp. 69-71; Milos Velimirovic, *Byzantine Elements in Early Slavic Chant*, Pars principalis, (Copenhagen: Monumenta Musicae Byzantinae, 1960), p. 38ff.

4. *Kontakion* (pl. *kontakia*) (τὸ κοντάκιον; кондакъ) and *oikos* (pl. *oikoi*) (οἶκος; ікосъ). In its initial form a kontakion was an extended poem that developed in detailed fashion the theme of the event or saint being celebrated. Unlike the kanon, the kontakion was not based on Old Testament themes. The poem contained as many as twenty-four metrically identical stanzas, oikoi, each of which ended with the same words. The first stanza of the kontakion, called the *prooemion* (προοίμιον) or *kukulion* (κουκούλιον), was different in metrical structure, but ended with the same refrain as the oikoi. This opening stanza briefly outlined the main theme of the entire poem, while the oikoi that followed developed the theme, sometimes in the form of a dialogue.[36] With the passage of time, however, the kontakion was abbreviated to the extent that only the kukulion and the first oikos remained. The term "kontakion" now was transfered to the kukulion while the first oikos maintained its original title of "oikos."

The most ancient Russian chant manuscripts already contain only these fragments of the original kontakion. Thus, for example, the sticherarion of the Chilandarian Fragments, a thirteenth-century manuscript, contains a kontakion (i.e., only the kukulion of the entire poem) and a first oikos for the Matins of Good Friday.[37]

Very few kontakia in today's liturgical books have preserved more than one oikos. For example, the kontakion of the last Sunday before Great Lent, the main theme of which is the expulsion of Adam from Paradise, has maintained, in addition to the kukulion, four oikoi, all of which are designated in the liturgical books as a single oikos, however. The full kontakion, including the kukulion and twenty-four oikoi, has been preserved in the rite for the burial of priests, while the rite for the burial of infants has also kept four oikoi.

The reduction of the full kontakion to only the kukulion and first oikos was due, most likely, to the increasing importance of the kanon, which began to supplant the kontakion in the ninth-tenth centuries. The remnants of the kontakion assumed a modest position following the sixth ode of the kanon.

In ancient times the kontakion was performed very solemnly by a solo singer who stood on the ambo.[38] Judging from ancient Russian manuscript sources, the melodies of the kontakia were quite melismatic and required a high degree of virtuosity on the part of the

[36] In English see Marjorie Carpenter, trans., *Kontakia of Romanos, Byzantine Melodist* (Columbia, Mo.: University of Missouri Press, 1970, 1973).

[37] *Fragmenta Chiliandarica, A. Sticherarium*, pp. 50v-51r.

[38] As late as the seventeenth century the ambo was a separate edifice in the center of the church and not part of the soleia, as it is today.

singer. This same fact makes it highly unlikely that the kontakia were ever performed by an ensemble, even singing in unison. A documented account relates that a singer who was about to sing the kontakion put on special vestments for the occasion and received a coin as a reward for his singing.[39] Another source explicitly states, however, that the final words of the kontakion for Good Friday were sung by the entire congregation; the solo singer evidently performed the bulk of the text, while the congregation participated by joining in singing the final words of the stanzas.[40]

The various kontakia, i.e. their kukulia, were collected in special books called *kontakaria* (κοντακάρια; кондакари). Among kontakaria of Russian origin there are only five such books known to exist today. These ancient kontakaria contain special musical notation (see Chapter III) that is markedly different from the one employed for writing down the melodies of stichera and heirmoi. This confirms that kontakia were performed in an entirely different manner than stichera and heirmoi. The special kontakarian notation, although still not conclusively deciphered, does indicate that the melodies for which it was used were highly complex and melismatic, and were performed with a variety of dynamic and technical vocal effects. Because this notation is found only in ancient Russian kontakaria, Razumovskii coined the term кондакарное знамя to describe the notation and кондакарное пение to describe the singing it expressed.[41] By the end of the thirteenth century, however, kontakarian singing had gradually lost its significance, and the notation faded from use and was forgotten.

Akathistos Hymn (ὁ Ἀκάθιστος ὕμνος; акафістъ, несѣдальное пѣніе).[42] The Akathistos Hymn is essentially a complete kontakion, consisting of a kukulion and twenty-four shorter stanzas with longer stanzas interspersed among them. In modern terminology the shorter stanzas are termed "kontakia" and end invariably with the refrain, "Alleluia," while the longer ones, ending with the same words as the kukulion, are termed "oikoi." The term "Akathistos Hymn" refers not to the literary or musical form of the poem or hymn,

---

[42] Egon Wellesz, *A History of Byzantine Music and Hymnography*, 2nd ed., (Oxford: Clarendon Press, 1962), p. 191.

[39] See Ivan A. Gardner, "Изображеніе св. Романа Сладкопевца как церковнаго певца" [The image of St. Romanos the Sweet-Singer as a church singer], Православная Жизнь (1964) No. 10, pp. 19-24.

[40] See n. 37.

[41] Nikolai D. Uspenskii, "Византийское пение в Киевской Руси" [Byzantine singing in Kievan Russia], *Acten des X. Internationalen Byzantinisten-Kongresses 1958* (Munich: 1960), pp. 643-654.

but rather, to the position of the congregation during its performance: during the performance the congregation must remain standing (hence the Greek ἀκάθιστος or the Slavonic несѣдальное, lit., "non-seated"). In this sense the Akathistos Hymn is the opposite of the sedalen.

The hymn being referred to here is the Akathistos Hymn to the Mother of God—the most ancient (seventh century) and authentic of such poems.[43] According to the Typikon it is to be performed at the Matins of Saturday of the fifth week of Great Lent, upon which occasion it is divided into four parts: each part begins and ends with the kukulion and contains three kontakia and three oikoi. The parts are performed, respectively: (a) After the first kathisma of the Psalter. (b) After the second kathisma.[44] (c) After the first group of odes of the kanon, i.e., after the third ode. (These three parts, therefore, are performed in the places where normally a sedalen would be performed.) (d) After the sixth ode of the kanon, where the modern shortened form of the kontakion is normally performed. In present-day practice the priest intones the text of the stanzas, while the refrain is sung by the choir, often joined by the entire congregation.

5. *Hypakoe* (ὑπακοή; ипакои). A stanza, similar in character to a troparion, that is performed at the Matins of Easter, Nativity and Theophany, in place of the sedalen, i.e., after the third ode of the kanon. The name refers to the style of performance: ὑπακούειν ="to listen," "to respond," or "to follow."[45] In the most ancient Russian manuscripts hypakoe were notated in kontakarian notation and possessed melodies of highly melismatic character.[46] It is likely that the performance of hypakoe originally involved the entire congregation, which followed a cantor or soloist, possibly in canonarchal style; but today the hypakoe is usually simply recited by a reader, having lost its initial liturgico-musical identity.

[43] This Akathistos Hymn was viewed as the classical model. Later, especially in the seventeenth, eighteenth and nineteenth centuries, the Russians composed numerous other akathistos hymns in honor of various icons of the Mother of God and various saints in imitation of this model. These later akathistos hymns, some of which are of rather low literary quality, may be included in private prayer services and, on occasion, into Vespers and Matins at the discretion of the rector. The Typikon prescribes only the original Akathistos Hymn.

[44] The order for reading the kathismas of the Psalter is given in the Typikon, chap. 17, pp. 30r-33r.

[45] Konstantin Nikol'skii, Пособие к изучению устава богослужения православной церкви [An aid to the study of the Typikon of the Orthodox Church], 6th ed., (St. Petersburg: 1908), p. 271 n.

[46] *Contacarium Mosquense*, p. 172ff.

6. *Antiphon* (τὸ ἀντίφωνον; антіфонъ). Antiphonal singing has already been discussed (pp. 31-32). From what has been said, it follows that an antiphon, generally speaking, is a hymn that is sung by two choirs in alternation. Specifically, the term "antiphon" applies to the following:

(a) The psalms performed verse by verse during the Liturgy of the Catechumens. (b) The first three "Glories" of the first kathisma at Saturday evening Vespers.[47] (c) Three troparion-like stanzas performed at resurrectional Matins before the reading of the Gospel; each stanza is sung by the right choir and repeated by the left. Each tone has three such antiphons, which consist of three stanzas, except tone 8, which contains four antiphons. These antiphons are also called graduals (ἀναβαθμοί; степенны), since their contents are based on Psalms 119-132, subtitled in the Psalter "Songs of Ascents." On days other than Sundays when the Gospel is to be read at Matins, the First Antiphon of the Fourth Tone, "From my youth," is always sung. Below is given the scheme for the correct performance of a gradual antiphon, using the First Antiphon of the Fourth Tone as an example:

1. Right Choir: From my youth many passions
                 Have fought against me.
                 But do Thou help me
                 And save me, O my Savior.

Repeated by Left Choir.

2. Right Choir: You who hate Zion.
                 Shall be put to shame by the Lord;
                 You shall be withered up
                 Like grass by the fire.

Repeated by Left Choir.

3. Right Choir: Glory to the Father and to the Son
                                and to the Holy Spirit.
                 Every soul is enlivened
                 By the Holy Spirit,
                 And is exalted in purity,
                 Illumined by the Holy Trinity
                 In a sacred mystery.

[47] Typikon, p. 3v.

Left Choir: Both now and ever and unto ages of ages, amen.
(Repeats third verse of antiphon.)

The gradual antiphons of each tone have distinctive melodies that belong only to them. (d) A fourth category is the troparion-like stanzas of varying length that are grouped into fifteen antiphons and performed at the Matins of Good Friday between the first five Gospel readings, three at a time. Each stanza is repeated by the opposite choir.[48]

7. *Prokeimenon* (τὸ προκείμενον; прокіменъ). Originally a larger section of a psalm (occasionally, an entire psalm), the prokeimenon today consists of only one or two verses of a given psalm that directly precede the reading of Holy Scripture. The performance of the prokeimenon represents a combination of antiphonal and responsorial styles: the reader announces the tone of the prokeimenon and intones the text of the first psalm verse; this verse is repeated by the right choir. The reader then intones the next psalm verse, which is answered with the original verse by the singers (the left choir, if two choirs are employed). In conclusion, the reader intones the first half of the original verse to which the singers respond with the second half of that verse. During the performance of a prokeimenon the reader must always be in the center of the church, while the singers are in their usual places.

There are two types of prokeimena: (a) Ordinary prokeimena consisting of two verses read by the reader, each answered by the choir in the manner described above. (b) Great prokeimena, which consist of four additional verses, each answered by singing the first verse. Great prokeimena end in the same manner as ordinary prokeimena, i.e. with the initial verse divided between the reader and the choir. These prokeimena are performed at Saturday evening Vespers ("The Lord is King...."), Vespers following Great Feasts of the Lord, and Sunday evening Vespers in Great Lent.

Prokeimena at the Divine Liturgy are related to the main theme of the occasion being celebrated. Thus, for example, the prokeimenon for the feast of Pentecost consists of the first half of verse 4 of Psalm 18 (in the eighth tone):

Their proclamation has gone out into all the earth,
And their words to the ends of the universe.

---

[48] The stanzas of these antiphons are also called "troparia" in liturgical singing-books. See Тріодъ постная [The Lenten Triodion], (Jordanville, N. Y.: Holy Trinity Monastery, 1956), p. 465.

The second (intervening) verse is verse 2 from the same psalm:

> Day to day pours forth speech, and night to night
> declares knowledge.

The reader then intones:

> Their proclamation has gone out into all the earth . . .

to which the choir answers:

> . . . and their words to the ends of the universe.

In addition to Liturgy prokeimena there are Vespers prokeimena (daily prokeimena) for each day of the week. These prokeimena remain the same from week to week, and are each connected with a specified tone and melody. At Matins, prokeimena are required only when there is a specified Gospel reading; the tones of the prokeimena change according to the feast.

The melodies of prokeimena are, as a rule, short and of syllabic-neumatic character.

8. *Alleluia* ('Αλληλούια; аллилуиарій). The alleluia precedes the reading of the Gospel at Divine Liturgy and hence, constitutes a prokeimenon to the Gospel.[49] It consists of the word "alleluia" repeated several times (usually three) with one or two intervening psalm verses intoned by the reader; textually the psalm verses relate to the event being celebrated. The performance of the alleluia is exactly the same as that of the prokeimenon, as illustrated below by the alleluia for the feast of the Ascension of the Lord:

Reader: Announces the number of the tone.

Choir: "Alleluia" three times in the announced tone.

Reader: God has gone up with a shout; the Lord, with the sound of a trumpet. (Psalm 46:6)

Choir: "Alleluia" three times.

Reader: Clap your hands, all peoples! Shout to God with loud songs of joy. (Psalm 46:2)

Choir: "Alleluia" three times.

---

[49] Present-day practice in the Russian Church often reduces the Alleluia to a three-fold repetition of the word "alleluia" sung to a plain melody instead of the prescribed tone. In this corrupt form the Alleluia appears to be merely

As with the prokeimenon, the performance of the alleluia can involve the entire congregation.

9. *Katabasia* (καταβασία, from καταβαίνω = "descend"; катавасia). Strictly speaking, the term "katabasia" refers to the coming together of both the right and left choir in the center of the church. In the thirteenth century the term applied to a number of hymns that were performed either by a solo singer who descended from the ambo for the performance or by both choirs which came down from their usual places and joined in the center of the church. Thus, for example, the Moscow (Uspenskii) Kontakarion of 1207 labels the following hymns "katabasia": "Calling the Magi by a star" [50] (in present-day terminology the hypakoe following the third ode of the kanon for the Nativity); "When Thou broughtest light" [51] (today the hypakoe following the third ode of the kanon for Theophany); "Before the dawn" [52] (the present-day hypakoe for Easter); and certain other hymns. Today the term "katabasia" refers to the heirmos of the kanon that concludes a given ode or group of odes.

10. *Exaposteilarion, photagogikon* (ἐξαποστειλάριον or φωταγωγικόν; эксапостиларій or свѣтиленъ). A troparion-like stanza sung at Matins preceding the Psalms of Praise (Psalms 148-150) and their stichera. The term comes from the Greek ἐξαποστέλλω = "send out" and refers, most likely, to the fact that a single singer was "sent out" from the choir to the center of the church or the ambo for the performance. Another explanation, that the exaposteilarion received its name from its contents (referring to the eleven exaposteilaria of the Resurrection, which speak of the sending out of the Apostles to preach the Gospel, is applicable only to those eleven exaposteilaria which are linked in content to the eleven Resurrection Gospels and the corresponding Gospel stichera. Obviously, the exaposteilaria of other feasts have events of the feast as their main themes.

The term photagogikon (cf. the Greek φῶς, "light") is also explained in terms of the content of the texts, which, in some cases, speak of light or enlightenment, e.g., the photagogikon for Theophany:

The Savior has appeared, grace and truth, in the streams

a finale to the reading of the Epistle and not a prokeimenon to the Gospel as it is intended to be.
[50] *Contacarium Mosquense*, p. 155r.
[51] Ibid., p. 161r.
[52] Ibid., p. 163v.

of the Jordan, and enlightened those who were in darkness and shadow: since the unapproachable Light has come
and appeared.

However, there are photagogika in which there is no mention what-
soever of light or enlightenment, e.g., the photagogikon for the Dormition:

O Apostles, gathered here from the ends of the earth,
bury my body in the garden of Gethsemane: and do Thou,
my Son and my God, receive my spirit.

Another possible explanation for the term is that the hymn was
performed at the end of Matins when daylight had already broken.

11. *Communion Hymn* (κοινωνικόν; причастенъ, кіноникъ).
A verse from a psalm (more rarely some other text from Holy Scripture) that is sung during the communion of the clergy and concludes
with an extended melismatic setting of the word "alleluia," sometimes repeated several times. The content of the verse is selected
in accordance with the theme of the day. For example, the communion hymn for the day of Pentecost is taken from the second half
of verse 10 of Psalm 142: "Let Thy good Spirit lead me on a level
path. Alleluia." Since the communion hymn must fill in the time
during which the clergy are receiving communion in the Sanctuary,
the chants of the communion hymns are quite melismatic. In ancient
kontakaria, the communion hymns were notated in kontakarian
notation, which suggests that they were performed in the complex
and virtuoso style characteristic of kontakarian singing.

12. *Magnification* (μεγαλυνάριον; величание). A short verse,
usually beginning with the word "magnify," sung in Slavic practice as
a hypophon to selected psalm verses after the Polyeleos at Matins on
Great Feasts and certain saints' days (See p. 80)
      Present-day practice, which includes freely-composed poly-
phonic choral music in the Western manner, has allowed the performance of hymns other than those prescribed by the Typikon during the
communion of the clergy. Very often these include heirmoi, stichera
and other verses that may or may not have anything in common with
the theme of a given day.
      All of the types of hymns and styles of performance described
above have a fixed and definite place in the liturgy and cannot be
rearranged or interchanged according to personal whim or preference.
The gradations of the musical element in the service and the sequence

and different combinations of hymns are carefully prescribed by the Typikon. This makes the service an integrated ideological and musical whole from a musical-literary point of view. As a result, the structure of the liturgy has a decisive influence on the style of performance and upon the extent and manner in which the musical element is employed. And it is for this reason that it is impossible to separate the liturgical singing of the Orthodox Church from the liturgy itself or to consider it exclusively in musical terms. The structure, forms and text of the liturgy exploit the musical element in accordance with a logical flow of ideas expressed by words and organized into a fixed liturgical format; the musical element flows out of the liturgy itself and constitutes an inseparable aspect of it.

Melodic Types: Idiomela, Automela, Prosomoia

From the standpoint of melodic origin, virtually all hymns sung to melodies found within the system of the eight tones, especially stichera, can be classified according to the following three groups:

1. *Idiomela* (ἰδιόμελα; самогласны), which possess their own intrinsic melodies and do not serve as models or patterns for other hymns of the same textual category. These include, for example, stichera of the Resurrection, stichera of Great Feasts, etc. Whether a given sticheron belongs to the category of idiomela is designated next to the text of the sticheron in the liturgical books.

2. *Automela* (αὐτόμελα; самоподобны), which also possess their own characteristic melodies, but serve as models (both melodic and metrical) for other hymns of the same tone and hymnographic category.

3. *Prosomoia* (προσόμοια; подобны), which follow the model of a given automelon both melodically and metrically.[53] The texts of Greek prosomoia have the same number of syllables as the corresponding automelon, which obviously simplifies the application of the melody of the latter to a new text. This relationship was not possible to maintain in translating the texts into Church Slavonic, however, and made the process of singing "to the automelon" (на самоподобен) much more difficult. It is reasonable to assume, therefore, that in order to preserve the principle of singing to the automelon, the

[53] For this reason a given sticheron-prosomoion that is to be sung to an automelon is always supplied with a designation of the first words of the automelon.

Russians were obliged to create new melodies for the automela that were more flexible than the Greek ones with regard to accommodating texts with varying numbers of syllables. And, in fact, the melodies of Russian automela tend to be more recitative-like, which enables them to be used for different texts with constantly changing numbers of syllables.[54]

The metrical and syllabic correlation between a Greek automelon and prosomoion is illustrated by the following example from the stichera aposticha of the Pre-Feast of the Nativity, "House of Ephratha" (in the second tone):

Automelon	Prosomoion	No. of syllables
1. Οἶκος τοῦ Εὐφραθᾶ	Ψάλλε προφητικῶς	6
2. Ἡ πόλις ἡ ἁγία	Δαβὶδ κινῶν τὴν λύραν	7
3. Τῶν προφητῶν ἡ δόξα	Τῆς σῆς γὰρ ἐξ ὀσφύος	7
4. Εὐπρέπισον τὸν οἶκον	Ἐξ ἧς ἡ θεοτόκος	7
5. Ἐν ᾧ τὸ θεῖον τίκτεται.	Χριστὸς γεννᾶται σήμερον.	8

It is noteworthy that virtually all textual stresses in the two texts fall in corresponding places.

A much different situation exists, however, when comparing the Slavonic translation of this automelon with a sticheron from the aposticha for the feast of Transfiguration which, according to the Typikon, is to be sung to the same automelon, "House of Ephratha": [55]

Automelon	No. of syllables	Prosomoion	No. of syllables
1. Доме Еврафовъ	5	Днесь Христосъ	3
2. Граде святый	4	На горѣ Ѳаворстѣй	6
3. Пророковъ славо	5	Адамово премѣнивъ	7
4. Украси домъ	4	Очернѣвшее естество	8
5. Въ немже божественный рождается	10	Просвѣтивъ богосодѣла	8

---

[54] Contemporary Russian liturgical service books without musical notation contain designations for sixty-one automela for stichera, forty-six for troparia and kontakia, and five for exaposteilaria; however, the corresponding singing-books contain only an insignificant fraction of these melodies (only for stichera), and the actual practice of singing to the automelon is even more rare, found only occasionally in monastic singing. See Ivan A. Gardner, "Забытое богатство (о пении на подобен)" [Forgotten treasure (concerning singing to the automelon)], Воскресное чтение (Warsaw), 1930, and published separately, 32 pp.

[55] An excellent example of singing to the automelon (with a canonarch) can be heard on the recording *Chants liturgiques russes*, in the series *L'Anthologie sonore* 1806 LD.

Here both the number of syllables and the relative position of accented and unaccented syllables show marked discrepancies between the automelon and prosomoion, as well as between the Greek original and the Slavonic translation. The example given here uses the current text utilized by the Russian Church; if, however, a text dating from before 1668 were used, in which the hard and soft signs, "ъ" and "ь," were pronounced as syllable-forming "o" and "e," the discrepancy would have been even greater.

Gradations of the Musical Element in the Liturgy

Inasmuch as the structure of the liturgy determines the use of various styles of performance, the musical element possesses no independent significance apart from the liturgy. The music does not exist side by side with the liturgical texts or side by side with liturgical actions. Rather, it exists within the liturgy, forming an intergrated whole.

In speaking of the musical setting of the word as it is presented to the listener, it is necessary to discuss in general terms the various degrees to which the musical element manifests itself in the liturgy. Obviously such a discussion cannot be limited to singing alone, for where does half-singing, recitation, or half-recitation leave off and true singing begin? The boundaries between them are very nebulous, especially when one considers such matters as recitative. Yet a great number of hymns are performed in recitative fashion. The following is an attempt to identify the various gradations of the musical element that are found in Orthodox worship.

As was observed earlier, the most primitive form of the musical element is recitation upon a single note, *recto tono*. Recitation, or psalmody, is distinguished from ordinary speech by the following features: (a) a constant level of pitch upon which the words are pronounced; (b) a slightly extended duration of the vowels, which, at the same time, remain rather constant in their dynamic level instead of being exploded as in ordinary speech. By comparison the duration of vowels in ordinary speech is relatively short: they are either articulated explosively or are imploded—"swallowed." The pitch of each vowel sound in ordinary speech may vary in spite of its brevity, changing even within the limits of a single vowel phoneme, and for this reason cannot be precisely determined. In psalmody, on the other hand, the pitch upon which the text is recited can be readily determined. While minute deviations from this basic pitch, often in micro-intervals, can be observed, particularly at the ends of text phrases, it is extremely difficult to express them precisely in terms of the equally-tempered scale. Numerous attempts to notate psalmody by means of the modern-day system of musical notation have all proven to be imprecise both in terms of rhythm and pitch.

Only at the end of a psalmodized text does the reader make significant deviations from the basic pitch, perhaps as large as a whole tone, at the same time prolonging certain syllables, but in a manner that cannot be accurately notated by means of proportionate note values. In general, the rhythmic definition of each syllable is negligible, since the recitation moves at a rate of approximately four to six syllables per second. Voiced consonants such as "m" and "n," if they are located between two other consonants (e.g., in the word празднство, "feast"), become almost separate syllables; the duration of such phonemes is indeterminable. Finally, in psalmody, as in ordinary speech, individual sounds are not subject to mutual temporal coordination.

This type of psalmody *recto tono* is common to all Christian churches having a hierarchy in the apostolic succession, regardless of the language employed, with only minor regional differences. From a purely musical standpoint the parts of the service performed in this manner represent "valleys" on the liturgico-musical curve, constituting periods of relative musical repose.

The next higher gradation of the musical element in the liturgy is ekphonesis (ἐκφώνησις; возгласъ),[56] which may be roughly translated as "exclamation." While this is still not singing in the full sense of the word, neither is it recitation *recto tono*. The level of the basic pitch is not as constant as in recitation. Ekphonesis exhibits definite deviations from the central pitch as large as a half- or whole-step up or down, as well as occasional larger intervals of deviation. In addition, the median pitch in ekphonesis is generally somewhat higher than in recitation. But most importantly, the vowels of certain syllables are prolonged and, on occasion, in accented syllables, take on mensural proportion (usually in a ratio of 2:1, or in a closing cadence even greater). The middle of the phrase is still recited on a single pitch, but the ends of phrases and especially the end of a complete text are virtually sung, with two- or three-note melismas possible on a given syllable. What distinguishes ekphonesis from

---

[56] Concerning ekphonesis see Carsten Høeg, *La notation ekphonétique* (Copenhagen: Monumenta Musicae Byzantinae, 1935); concerning present-day Russian ekphonesis, see Hieromonk Gerontii (Kurganovskii), Метод богослужебных возгласов, положенных на ноты [The method of liturgical exclamations set to music], (Moscow: Синодальная типография, 1897).

singing proper is that the melodic characteristics occur only at the ends of phrases, while the main portion of the text is recited. Ekphonesis itself exhibits several gradations. In its least-developed form it is little distinguished from psalmody, while on the other end of the spectrum it takes on many characteristics of singing. This makes the dividing line between ekphonesis and singing quite nebulous. In fact, in such cases as the *lectio solemnis* of the Greek, Serbian, Bulgarian and certain other churches, ekphonesis displays bona fide characteristics of singing not only at the ends of phrases but also at their beginning.

By contrast to ekphonesis, in singing virtually every vowel sound is performed on a distinct and precisely determinable pitch,[57] forming a more or less continuous melodic line. The duration of the pitches can also be measured in relation to some fundamental unit of time, and thus can be written down by means of traditional musical notation. A definite rhythm can be perceived, whether it is free, determined by the accentuation of the text, or symmetrical, exhibiting periodicity of alternating strong and weak beats. Furthermore, in singing several pitches of varying height and duration frequently fall on a single syllable of text, forming a melisma, which in ekphonesis occurs only in exceptional cases.

The principal gradations of the musical element in liturgy are summarized in the following table:

Recitation-Psalmody	*Ekphonesis*	*Singing*
Constant level of pitch; mensurably indeterminable duration of individual syllables; slight elongation of vowels; deviations from the basic pitch only at the ends of phrases or texts; lack of clear rhythm; virtually no variation in dynamic level.	Constant level of pitch with likely deviations at the beginnings and especially the ends of phrases and texts; level of median pitch somewhat higher than in psalmody; more extensive elongation of vowels but still without a clearly distinguishable rhythm; small changes in dynamics possible; occasional short melismas, especially at ends of phrases.	Varying levels of pitch over individual syllables; clearly distinguishable intervals; variable duration of pitches that can be more or less precisely determined; more frequent melismas; clearly discernible rhythm; tempo and dynamic level can exhibit marked changes.

[57] In accordance with the tonal system. For example, in Greek (late-Byzantine) liturgical chanting many intervals in certain tones do not exactly correspond to the half- and whole-steps of the modern equally-tempered scale. See J. B. Rebours, *Traité de psaltique* (Paris: Alphonse Picar & fils and Leipzig: Otto Harrassovits, 1906), pp. 35-68.

The System of Eight Tones

For all the various national branches of the Orthodox Church there exists a single system that governs the order and style of performance of liturgical singing. At a certain point in history the Russian Church inherited this system from the Greek Church of Constantinople as the guiding principle for the musical organization of the liturgy. The system, which is common not only to the Eastern Orthodox churches but also to the Roman Catholic and to certain other non-Orthodox Eastern churches, is the Oktoechos (ὀκτώηχος; осмогласие), a system of eight musical modes or tones (ἤχοι; гласы; Latin: *toni*) that contain all the melodies of canonical liturgical singing. Most liturgical hymns, whether found in musically notated liturgical books or in those without musical notation, are supplied with a designation of the tone in which the hymn is to be performed. When the liturgical books were translated from Greek to Church Slavonic in the earliest formative stages of the Russian Church, these designations of the tone were retained.

According to the rules set down in the Typikon, the services of each week of the liturgical year are governed alternately by one of the eight tones. This governance begins at Saturday evening Vespers and extends through the Ninth Hour of the following Saturday. In this way there arises a rotating eight-week-long cycle of tones, the so-called "Pillar of Tones" (гласовой столп).[58] The Pillar begins with the first tone on the second Sunday after Pentecost, and ends with Vespers of the last Saturday before Great Lent. The end of the cycle applies only to the weekdays of Great Lent, however. For Sundays the cycle continues until the fifth Sunday of Great Lent. Thus, the liturgical year contains approximately six Pillars.

The cycle can be interrupted by the occurrence of Great Feasts. The services of these feasts have their own combinations of tones, which have precedence over the prevailing tone of the week. Also, at various times hymns that are governed by the tone of the week may be supplemented or supplanted by hymns from the monthly cycle, the Menaion, for which there may be specified tones other than the prevailing tone of the week.[59]

[58] There is also an eleven-week Pillar consisting of the eleven Resurrection Gospel readings at Matins and the corresponding exaposteilaria and Gospel stichera. To distinguish it from the Pillar of Eight Tones, it is termed the "Gospel Pillar" (евангельский столп). The Gospel Pillar can never exactly coincide with the Pillar of Eight Tones.

[59] The hymns for each day of the week in each tone are contained in a

The texts of the hymns in the eight-week Pillar of Tones are unique to each of the tones. This is a significant factor, since there occur instances in which a melody for a certain hymn may be composed outside of the compass of the tone. In this case the designation of the tone continues to apply to the text but not to its musical setting. For example, the stichera on the Beatitudes were occasionally sung in *demestvenny* style, found in Russia during the sixteenth and seventeenth centuries, which lies outside the cycle of eight tones. If the texts of these stichera were not designated by the tone to which they belonged, it would be impossible to identify the text in question.

Occasionally, liturgical books omit a designation of the tone for certain hymns. Most often this occurs in the case of unchanging hymns of the Divine Liturgy and Vigil, such as "O Gladsome Light," "Only-Begotten Son," the Cherubic Hymn, etc. This means that the given hymn lies outside of the system of tones and may either be performed to a melody of any tone desired or to one or several freely-composed melodies that bear no relation to the Oktoechos.

Greek liturgical music books containing staffless neumatic notation always contain a designation of tone, however, even for the unchanging hymns mentioned above. This is true even if several different musical settings for the same hymn are given. This has led certain writers to assert that only singing based on the Oktoechos can be considered liturgical.[60] On the basis of this assertion they conclude that if a certain liturgical text is set to a melody lying outside the Oktoechos (e.g. in *demestvenny* style), such singing can no longer be viewed as liturgical, but rather, as "domestic singing" not suitable for the Church. This viewpoint, however, must be reexamined in light of the fact that in the Greek system of musical notation the designation of the tone was absolutely essential. Without it the singer did not know within which structure of intervallic relationships he was to execute a given melody notated in staffless neumes. An analogous situation would exist with a passage rendered in conventional Western European notation if the key signature were omitted. The designation of the tone in Byzantine music served as a type of key

---

book called the *Oktoechos* ('Οκτώηχος; октоихъ, осмогласникъ, октай). The hymns for each day of the year, i.e., those connected specifically with a given date (non-movable feasts, commemoration of saints, etc.), are contained in the Menaion (минеа), also known as the Menologion (Μηνολόγιον; минологий).

[60] See, for example, Razumovskii, *op. cit.*, pp. 181-184; I. I. Voznesenskii, О церковном пении православной греко-российской церкви: Большой и малый знаменный роспев [Concerning the church singing of the Orthodox Graeco-Russian Church. The Great and Little Znamenny Chant], Vols. I and II, (Riga: 1890), pp. 15-17.

signature that made possible the correct rendition of a given musical passage.

The staffless liturgical singing books of the Russian Church, particularly those of the sixteenth and seventeenth centuries, also contain a number of hymns—stichera—that were performed in several tones, changing or alternating in the course of a single hymn. Such hymns are found in Greek singing books as well. Depending on the number of changing tones these hymns are called *oktaechon* (ὀκτάηχον; осмогласникъ) with the order: 1-5-2-6-3-7-4-8-1 [61] or 1-2-3-4-5-6-7-8-1, or *tetraechon* (τετράηχον; четверогласникъ) with the order: 5-6-7-8.[62]

In the Russian system of eight tones there is no musical relationship between the authentic tones and their plagal counterparts. The principle of pairing tones 1 and 5, 2 and 6, 3 and 7, and 4 and 8, which does exist in the Byzantine system, was copied by the Russians in a purely external fashion. In connection with this it must be pointed out that there is a significant difference between the system of grouping tones (or modes) in the Eastern Orthodox Chuch and the system employed in the Western Roman Catholic Church, although both systems follow the principle of pairing. The table below illustrates the principal differences between the two systems:

Byzantine system	*Gregorian system*
Tone (Mode) 1. (ἦχ. α΄) Authentic	Dorian (Authentic)
Tone (Mode) 2. (ἦχ. 6΄) Authentic	Hypo-Dorian (Plagal)
Tone (Mode) 3. (ἦχ. γ΄) Authentic	Phrygian (Authentic)
Tone (Mode) 4. (ἦχ. δ΄) Authentic	Hypo-Phrygian (Plagal)
Tone (Mode) 5. (ἦχ. πλ. α΄) Plagal of 1	Lydian (Authentic)
Tone (Mode) 6. (ἦχ. πλ. 6΄) Plagal of 2	Hypo-Lydian (Plagal)
Tone (Mode) 7. (ἦχ. πλ. γ΄) Plagal of 3	Mixolydian (Authentic)
Tone (Mode) 8. (ἦχ. πλ. δ΄) Plagal of 4	Hypo-Mixolydian (Plagal)

Thus, in the Byzantine system the pairing between authentic and plagal modes follows the order 1-5, 2-6, 3-7, and 4-8, while in the Gregorian system, the order is 1-2, 3-4, etc. In Byzantine nomenclature tones 5, 6, and 8 are not designated by their numbers, but

[61] E.g., Μουσικὸς Πανδέκτις, Τόμος ε΄, Μέρος Α΄. (Athens: Zoe, 1937), p. 399.
[62] E.g., in the MS found in the State and University Library of Breslau, Slav. 5, p. 481v.

rather, as plagal of the first (πλάγιος πρώτου), plagal of the second (πλάγιος δευτέρου), and plagal of the fourth (πλάγιος τετάρτου), respectively. By way of exception, tone 7 is not designated as the plagal of the third, but as ἦχος βαρύς—the grave tone. In contrast to Byzantine and Gregorian nomenclature, the Russian system does not employ the terms "authentic" and "plagal," but uses only numbers to designate the various tones (гласы). In ancient Russian musical monuments even tone 7 is designated by the number. Only in a single instance is tone 7 designated as the grave tone—гласъ тяжькъ.[63]

As far as the relationship between authentic and plagal tones in the Russian system is concerned, the question still requires a good deal of investigation. It appears that if there were musical correlations between them in the earliest period of liturgical singing in Russia (a fact that cannot be either proved or disproved at present), with the course of time these correspondences became obscured to such a degree that today these paired tones only have in common certain melodic patterns.

In general, the tonal and structural features that distinguish one tone from another in the system of ancient Russian singing have not yet been determined with sufficient clarity. The theories of IU. Arnol'd [64] as well as those of Razumovskii, based on ancient Greek modes, yield irresolvable conflicts and contradictions when applied to the analysis of ancient Russian canonical melodies, especially those of Znamenny Chant. Similar problems plague the theoretical efforts of I. Voznesenskii, who based his work in part on that of Arnol'd.[65] None of these works can serve as valid points of departure for present-day efforts to determine the theoretical basis of classifying the distinctions between the Russian ecclesiastical tones.

[63] E.g., in the Sinai Euchologion, a Slavonic *trebnik* of the tenth century written in the Glagolithic alphabet. See Rajko Nachtigal, *Euchologium Sinaiticum*, 2 vols. (Ljubliana: 1941, 1942), vol. 1, p. 97; vol. 2, p. 301. See also, V. Metallov, Русская семиография [Russian semeiography], (Moscow: 1912), Plate VIII.

[64] IU. Arnol'd, Гармонизация древне-русского церковного пения по эллинской и византийской теории и по акустическому анализу [The harmonization of ancient Russian liturgical singing according to Hellenic and Byzantine theory and acoustical analysis] (Moscow: 1886). IU. Arnol'd, Теория православного церковного пения вообще, по учению эллинских и византийских писателей [The general theory of Orthodox liturgical singing according to Hellenic and Byzantine writers], (Moscow, 1880).

[65] I. Voznesenskii, Большой и малый знаменный роспев [The Great and Little Znamenny Chant], (Riga: 1890).

The Aesthetics of Liturgical Singing

From everything said in this chapter thus far, it is evident that the liturgical singing of the Orthodox Church has its own particular aesthetic laws, which determine the realization of the musical element in the liturgy and the forms of liturgical singing in a manner quite different from the realm of secular music. The musical element is manifested and utilized in the following ways:

1. In varying gradations of the musical element, integrally connected with the word: recitation *recto tono*, ekphonesis, and singing, with the latter varying from recitative to highly developed melismatic style.

2. In varying styles of performance: solo, choral, combined solo-choral, antiphonal-responsorial, hypophonic-epiphonic.

3. In the performance of singing and recitation in different locations in the church: in the special places assigned for the choir, in the center of the church, on the ambo, in the Sanctuary,[66] during processions both inside and outside of the church.

4. In various tones and melodic types.

All of these elements are arranged in the liturgy according to precise rules and regulations. In spite of their variety, they are tightly bound to one another, constituting an ever-changing yet continuous "curve of mood" or "curve of solemnity" in harmony with the liturgical calendar. Thus out of the many composite parts is formed one liturgico-musical, didactic and prayerful whole—the liturgy itself.

In the realm of vocal music the liturgical singing of the Orthodox Church constitutes an autonomous realm that is guided by its own aesthetic laws and standards. It is self-evident that it would be a grave mistake to expect or demand from liturgical singing the same forms and genres that are found in secular music or even in religious music that is separated from worship. The intermingling of these two realms can lead, on the one hand, to misunderstandings concerning liturgical singing, expecting from it that which it is not meant to contain, and, on the other hand, to the introduction of foreign elements into the liturgy that can subtly and gradually distort both the forms of liturgical singing and the very essence of the liturgy, resulting, once again, in an erroneous appraisal of its forms and aesthetic principles.

It is often remarked that Orthodox liturgical forms, both poetic and musical, have become frozen in time to the extent that all further

---

[66] E.g., during a Pontifical Divine Liturgy.

development and creativity have ceased. Such a view, however, does not correspond to reality. To be sure, the framework and structure of the liturgy have remained constant. But at the same time, a certain periodic fluctuation between periods of heightened creativity and decline can be observed, and even in times of relative decline there is evidence of continuing development. Within the unchanging framework there is always a certain amount of freedom for individual musical interpretation. And with the passage of time even the fixed structure of liturgical forms and styles of performance does not remain unchanged. Over the centuries many forms have lost their significance, having been supplanted by new ones. Styles of performance that were of paramount importance have given way to others that until then had been little-used. Such changes take place extremely slowly and can go unnoticed for several generations. Only given a long-term historical perspective can one observe and study the constant and gradual cycles of the flowering and decline of liturgico-musical art.

In spite of numerous obstacles and complications, liturgical singing among Orthodox Eastern Slavs developed continuously from 988, the year of the conversion of the Rus', to 1917, the year of the Russian Revolution. And it was in the Eastern Slavic branch of the Church that liturgical singing underwent the greatest and most radical changes over a period of a thousand years. These changes affected the most fundamental concepts concerning the essence and nature of liturgical singing, which, in turn, affected singing in other parts of the Orthodox world. Similar ideological changes affected developments in other areas of liturgical art, such as iconography and architecture. Throughout history, religious art reflected the "spirit of the age," which often was shaped or caused by circumstances external to the religious realm.

National Differences

While the essence of liturgical singing and the employment of the musical element in the liturgy are in principle the same for all the national branches of the Orthodox Church, the musical forms and the actual system of liturgical singing can vary considerably from one local national church to another. This diversity comes about as a result of such factors as historical conditions, local musical customs, influences from outside the Church and the overall musical sensibility of a given nationality. Specifically, the diversity manifests itself in the variety of musical styles and forms—melodic forms and modal structures that are intimately connected with language—as well as such aspects as the predominance of unison singing versus Western-style polyphony.[67] This multiplicity of forms exists in spite of the fact that the national branches of the Church utilize the same liturgical texts as the Byzantine Mother Church, simply translating them into the native language of the given country.

Since liturgical singing consists essentially of the word emotionally colored by means of musical sounds, it is evident that the musical element is determined by the word and the ideas which it expresses. Consequently, in each national manifestation of the Church the musical element is significantly affected by the peculiarities of vocal articulation and the natural rhythm of the given language. These factors vary not only from one nation to another, but even within various ethnic subgroups of the same nationality. Moreover, they may become altered with the passage of time—a factor that too often escapes the attention of the researcher. These regional influences are sometimes so strong that a certain melody borrowed from another ethnic subgroup of the same nationality may become inevitably altered as a result of local pronunciation and manner of voice production.[68]

Since the hymnography of the Orthodox Church is also dependent to a considerable extent upon dogmatic content, the translation of hymns and prayers must be made with the greatest precision in order to avoid categorically ambiguities and misrepresentations in the original hymnographer's dogmatic thinking. Errors in this regard can lead to heterodox concepts and ideas. For the same reason it is impossible to accept free translations that are not dogmatically precise, even though they might be more graceful from a literary and stylistic point of view.

Historically, when the Russians received Christianity from the

[67] In the Greek Church, for example, the singing is performed by solo singers or in unison by several of the best-trained singers, while the other singers, or the entire congregation, hold a drone pitch, the ison (ἴσον). By contrast, the Russians have employed polyphonic choral singing based on the principles of Western harmony since the seventeenth century. Russian Old Believers, on the other hand, permit only strict unison singing.

[68] The vocal placement and the articulation of consonants of the Greeks is markedly different from that of the Russians even in ordinary speech. (The voice "sits" differently.) The displacement of accents that inevitably occurred in the course of translating liturgical texts from Greek to Slavonic also resulted in rhythmic changes in the melodies that were adopted together with the texts. Among Northern and Northeastern Russians, low and rich voices predominate, while among the Southern Slavs higher and lighter voices are more numerous. This circumstance, together with the multiplicity of liturgical languages, also precludes a uniform approach to realizing the musical element in the liturgy.

Greeks, making not only translations of the texts but also borrowing the melodies of the hymns themselves, great care was taken to achieve the closest possible correlation in the number of syllables with the original. However, discrepancies in syllabification inevitably arose, resulting even then in a certain alteration of the melodic and rhythmic features of the original.

The differences between languages created enormous obstacles for the preservation of uniform liturgical singing in all of the multi-lingual national branches of the Orthodox Church. No comparable difficulty existed, for example, in the Roman Catholic Church with its uniform use of the Latin language. The thousand-year history of Orthodoxy among the Slavic peoples alone, not to mention the nine centuries of the Byzantine experience prior to that, has shown that every nation formulates the musical element differently, in accordance with its own liturgical language. For this reason it is not possible to speak of the liturgical singing of the entire Orthodox Church in general, all-inclusive terms.

The emotional reaction of the listener to the ideas expressed by the text, which, in turn, determines the forms of the musical element, depends on two other aspects: (a) the religious character of a given people, and (b) the particular nation's musical feeling. Thus, a somber penitential text may be set to an austere diatonic melody in Northern Russia, while Ukrainians would express it in a tender harmonic minor mode; among the Greeks still another setting would be found, using the chromatic sixth tone, with its irrational intervals. While these may be extreme examples, they serve to illustrate the nature of the diversity.

Liturgical singing can also be influenced by secular folk melodies and religious, but not liturgical, folk music and poetry, as well as by artistic creations imported and adapted for the liturgy. The character and scope that such influences may have had in earlier centuries can be determined only approximately, however. It is often impossible to establish where and in what manner a shift from the liturgical to secular musical orientation may have entered liturgical singing.

Summary

To summarize, the forces which generate the musical element in the liturgy of the Orthodox Church are as follows:

1. *The word*—liturgical texts that clearly and unambiguously

express concrete ideas in the various liturgical languages of the different national branches of the Church.

2. *The order of the liturgy*, which regulates the place and style in which the texts are performed as well as their liturgical function—narrative, praise, contemplation, etc.—in conjunction with various liturgical actions.

3. *The musical element per se*, including characteristics of the human voice, the laws of acoustics, etc.

Thus it is clear that it is not sufficient to view the study of Orthodox liturgical singing exclusively as a branch of musicology on the grounds that liturgical singing is vocal music and operates within a musical realm. Such an assertion would be valid if one were dealing with a purely musical phenomenon. However, the musical element in the liturgy is controlled and shaped by the word; music does not exist in the liturgy independent of the word, and it is dependent upon the content and position of different hymns in the liturgy. Consequently, one must also examine liturgical singing from other, non-musical aspects such as linguistics and liturgical archeology. This will be done in the succeeding chapters.

CHAPTER II

The Liturgical System of The Orthodox Church

As follows from the preceding chapter, the forms of liturgical singing in the Orthodox Church are closely connected with the order of worship. The order of worship is the context in which the "pictures"—the hymns in all their variety—are framed, thereby deriving their proper function. It is necessary, therefore, to examine this order more closely, at least in its main features.

To consider the entire history of the development of the order of worship and its parallels to the liturgical forms of the Western Church or other non-Orthodox Eastern Churches (e.g. Armenian, Coptic) would go beyond the scope of the present work. Such a task falls in the realm of liturgics and liturgical archeology.[1] Here we can only examine the structural aspect of worship with all essential brevity, discussing the exact structure of those services in which singing occupies a position of primary importance, and only briefly mentioning the offices that consist primarily of psalmodized and recited material.

The order of worship that serves today as the governing basis for all the services of the Russian Church [2] is the so-called Hagiopolitical-Hagiooritical order, used in Jerusalem (the Holy City) and on Mount Athos (the Holy Mountain). While it is used by the Russians in monastery, cathedral and parish churches alike,[3] this Typikon contains instructions intended specifically for monastery churches

---

[1] See, e.g., A. Baumstark, *Liturgie comparée*, 3rd ed. (Chevetogne, Belgium: 1953), and bibliography there (pp. 223-259); for the present-day liturgical order of the Russian Orthodox Church, see: K. Nikol'skii, Пособие к изучению устава Богослужения Православной Церкви [An aid to the study of the Typikon of the Orthodox Church], 6th ed. (St. Petersburg: n.p. 1900; reprint ed., Graz: Akademische Druck- und Verlagsanstalt, n.d.); S. V. Bulgakov, Настольная книга для священноцерковнослужителей [Reference book for the clergy], 2nd ed. (Kharkov: n.p. 1900; reprint ed., Graz: n.p. 1965); L. Mirkovic, Православна литургіка или наука о богослуженю православне источне цркве [Orthodox liturgics or the study of the liturgy of the Orthodox Church], vol. 1 (n.p., 1919; reprint ed., Belgrade: n.p. 1965).

[2] Типікон, сіесть уставъ, (Moscow: Синодальная типография, 1906; reprint ed., Moscow: n.p. 1954).

[3] The present-day Greek Orthodox Patriarchate of Constantinople, as well as the Bulgarian Orthodox Church, employs a different Typikon, which differs in many details of liturgical order from the Hagiopolitical-Hagiooritical order.

and calls for a maximum that can practically be performed only in larger monasteries. What is taken for granted in monasteries, however, becomes impossible in the daily lives of ordinary city dwellers. One simply cannot expect lay people with professional and family obligations to devote often as many as ten hours a day to church attendance. For this reason, abbreviations of the extremely long services are inevitably made in the practice of cathedral and parish churches. Since the Typikon itself contains no guidelines for such abbreviations, they are made according to local practice, taking some of the following forms: (a) the deletion of certain parts of services, especially those that are psalmodized or recited; (b) the omission of entire hymns, primarily those that are repeated several times, in which case the hymn is performed only once;[4] (c) the employment of shorter and simpler melodic settings; (d) reciting certain hymns that, according to the Typikon, are to be sung; (e) entirely omitting certain offices. It must be admitted, however, that such abbreviations are not always made correctly from a liturgical standpoint.

Although the Typikon represents a standard of maximum liturgical practice, at times there occur certain deviations from it in the practice of the largest and oldest monasteries and a few old cathedrals. These deviations, affecting both the hymns themselves and the manner in which they are performed, often represent the surviving remnants of older liturgical practices.

The order of worship found today in monasteries, cathedrals, and parish churches alike was definitively established sometime in the fifteenth century.[5] Prior to that, from the beginning of the Russian Church, the order of Constantinople had been employed: cathedrals employed the order of the St. Sophia Cathedral in Constantinople (τῆς μεγάλης ἐκκλησίας), while in monasteries the order of the Monastery of the Studios, also located in Constantinople, was used. The Constantinopolitan order of service differed from the Hagio-political-Hagiooritical order in a number of elements related to church singing. But only a few traces of it still remain today, and only in particular offices (e.g. the Matins of Holy Saturday).

The Daily Cycle of Services

The liturgical day of the Orthodox Church begins with Vespers—

---

[4] According to the Typikon, certain festal stichera are to be repeated twice or three times.
[5] Under Metropolitan Kiprian (1381-1385 and 1390-1406) and Metropolitan Fotii (1410-1431).

approximately at sunset. Thus the Vespers of Saturday evening belongs to Sunday, and therefore it has a festal character. The day ends with the Ninth Hour, which is celebrated immediately before the Vespers of the following day.

The liturgical day consists of the following offices:

1. Vespers (ἑσπερινός; вечерня)
2. Compline (ἀπόδειπνον; повечерие, павечерница)
3. Nocturn (μεσονυκτικόν; полунощница)
4. Matins (ὄρθρος; утреня)[6]
5. First Hour (α' ὥρα; первый час)
6. Third Hour (γ' ὥρα; третий час)
7. Sixth Hour (ϛ' ὥρα; шестой час)
8. Divine Liturgy (ἡ θεία λειτουργία; божественная литургия, обедня)
9. Ninth Hour (η' ὥρα; девятый час).

It is often the practice of cathedrals and parish churches to omit Compline, Nocturn, and Ninth Hour;[7] these services are celebrated only in monasteries.

In monastic practice these nine services are frequently arranged in three groups: (1)Ninth Hour, Vespers, and Compline—celebrated in the evening; (2) Nocturn, Matins, and First Hour — celebrated either at night or shortly before sunrise; and (3) Third Hour, Sixth Hour, and Divine Liturgy—celebrated before midday.[8] On the eves of major feasts (in Russian practice, every Saturday as well) the services of Vespers, Matins, and First Hour are combined to form what is referred to as the All-Night Vigil (ἀγρυπνία; всенощное бдение, or simply всенощная), which, celebrated in full, may literally last through the night.[9] In cathedral and parish churches this group of services is usually celebrated in greatly abbreviated form on Saturdays and the eves of major feasts.[10]

[6] Also заутреня; corresponds to Matins and Lauds of the Western Church.

[7] With the exception of Great Lent and the eves of the Nativity and the Theophany.

[8] In cathedrals and parish churches the following schedule is usually observed: evening—Vespers, early morning—Matins and First Hour, before midday—Third Hour, Sixth Hour, and Divine Liturgy.

[9] In monastic practice, on Sundays and feast days, when the All-Night Vigil is prescribed, the order of evening services is altered somewhat: after the Ninth Hour, the service of Little Vespers is celebrated. Then, after evening meal-time, Compline is performed.

[10] In Greek practice, Divine Liturgy is celebrated directly following Matins (through the Great Doxology), served early in the morning.

The All-Night Vigil also usually contains a Litiia (λιτή; литія), which is inserted into the second half of Vespers. The Litiia either takes the form of a procession around the church building and into the narthex, or is held in the narthex or extreme rear of the church.

Deviations from the usual format of daily offices occur in connection with feasts or at other special times of the year, such as Great Lent. Specifically, the weekdays of Great Lent, Holy Week, Easter Week (Bright Week), as well as the eves of the Nativity and Theophany, have a special order of offices. During Great Lent, for example, weekday Divine Liturgy (i.e. Presanctified) can be connected directly with Vespers, with the latter flowing into Liturgy without any distinct break. The structure of these special offices will be discussed in greater detail below.

Not all of the offices mentioned above are equally rich in terms of sung material. The Hours, for example, are in almost all cases recited; Compline and Nocturn also contain very few hymns that are sung. By contrast, Vespers (with Litiia) and Matins, especially when combined in the form of an All-Night Vigil, are particularly rich in sung material. Here, as nowhere else, appears the greatest variety of performance styles and types of hymns. These services consist primarily of hymns, the texts of which are at once devotional and develop the principal theme of the day or feast. The hymns are performed in various tones and musical styles, which results in a great deal of musical variety.

For each day, the hymnographical material that is sung and recited changes (a) according to the yearly cycle, and (b) according to the weekly cycle. In addition, at the appropriate periods it changes according to the Triodion cycle (which governs the period of Great Lent, Holy Week, and the four Sundays before Great Lent), and the Pentecostarion cycle (which extends from Easter Sunday to the first Sunday after Pentecost). The yearly cycle governs the hymns for each day of the month and is concerned with various fixed feasts and the commemoration of saints.[11] The hymns of this cycle are performed in various prescribed tones: e.g. different hymns in honor of St. Nicholas (December 6) are sung in every tone with the exception of tone seven. Other feasts and commemorations have their own prescribed patterns of tones.[12]

The weekly (or Oktoechos) cycle contains hymns for each day

---

[11] The yearly cycle is also referred to as the Menaion cycle (минейный круг), i.e., the monthly cycle.

[12] E.g., for the commemoration of Sts. Peter and Paul (June 29), the hymns are also sung in all the tones with the exception of tone seven, but in a different combination than for the commemoration of St. Nicholas.

of the week as well as for Saturday evening Vespers in each of the eight tones, forming the eight-week Pillar of Tones (гласовой столп). Hymns of the weekly cycle are combined in a given office with hymns from the yearly cycle according to specific rules, so that the musical form of each service displays a continuously changing array of melodies in various church tones.

Just as for the offices of the Western Church, the sung material of each Orthodox office may be divided into the following four categories:

1. Hymns of the ordinary: Unchanging material that constitutes the invariable framework of a given office. This material does not depend upon the feast days, tones, or days of the week, although the style or manner of performance may change depending on the occasion (festal, plain, or recited).

2. Material that remains constant for a particular office on a particular day of the week, regardless of the governing tone of the week, but changes with each day of the week without consideration for other factors (e.g. daily Vespers prokeimena).

3. Material that is employed only on special occasions, but is employed consistently on such occasions, regardless of the day of the week or the governing tone of the week (e.g. the Polyeleos). Such hymns may be classified as "occasional" hymns of the ordinary.

4. Propers: Materials that change for every day of the week and for every day of the year, either according to the governing tone or independently of it. The propers are interpolated into the unchanging framework formed by the ordinaries. One can liken the ordinaries to an ever-constant picture frame in which the picture—the propers—is changed daily.

There are some ordinaries whose text remains the same within the scheme of a given office, but which are performed in different tones, depending on the day of the week or the prevailing tone of the week. Such is the case, for example, with the Vespers Psalms (141, 129 and 116) and the Psalms of Praise (148, 149 and 150) of Matins.[13]

Given below are the outlines of the most important Orthodox services, together with some specific variants for special occasions.

Vespers

There are three varieties of Vespers:

[13] These psalms are sung in the tone of the first interpolated sticheron.

1. Great Vespers, celebrated on Saturday evenings and on the eves of major feasts as a component of the All-Night Vigil.
2. Daily Vespers
3. Little Vespers

For comparison, the outlines of Great Vespers and Daily Vespers are given side by side, followed separately by the outline for Little Vespers.

Great Vespers	*Daily Vespers*
1. Psalm 103—sung, possibly in hypophonal style.	1. Psalm 103—recited.

2. The Great Litany [14]—performed responsorially, combining ekphonesis of the deacon with the sung responses of the congregation or choirs, and closing with the doxology of the priest.

3. The first antiphon of the first kathisma of the Psalter — performed hypophonically or antiphonally. (On Saturday all three antiphons are performed, with Little Litanies inserted between them.)	3. One of the kathismas of the Psalter—recited.

4. Little Litany.

5. The Vespers Psalms — 140, 141, 129, and 116 — performed hypophonically or antiphonally in the prescribed tone of the Oktoechos.

---

[14] The litanies or ektenias (συναπταί; ектеніи or τὰ διακονικά; діаконства) consist of a series of petitions intoned by the deacon (or the priest, if there is no deacon serving). To each petition the congregation or the choir, which represents the congregation, answers with the response, "Lord, have mercy" (Κύριε ἐλέησον; Господи помилуй) or "Grant it, O Lord" (Παράσχου Κύριε; подай Господи). The following types of litanies are found in Orthodox services: (1) The Great Litany (великая ектенія), or the Litany of Peace (τὸ εἰρηνικὸν; мирная ектенія), which has twelve petitions, answered by "Lord, have mercy"; (2) The Little Litany (малая ектенія), which has only two petitions, answered by the same response; (3) The Augmented Litany (or Litany of Fervent Supplication) (сугубая ектенія) in which the number of petitions varies in different cases, but for which the response is a three-fold "Lord, have mercy"; (4) The Litany of Supplication (просительная ектенія), for which the first several petitions are answered with "Lord,

Between the last eight or ten verses of the psalm group, eight or ten stichera are inserted (depending on the occasion), performed in canonarchal style. For the performance of the last four (or three) stichera both choirs come together in the center of the church. The last one or two stichera are performed in a particularly festive manner. During the singing of the final sticheron the clergy make a solemn entrance into the Sanctuary through the Royal Doors.

Between the last six verses of the psalm group, six stichera are inserted, performed in canonarchal style.

6. The Evening Hymn, "O Gladsome Light"—sung in a festive manner by both choirs combined.

6. The Evening Hymn, "O Gladsome Light"—sung in a simple manner or recited.

7. Prokeimenon of the day—sung in responsorial-antiphonal style.

On the eves of feast days, the prokeimenon is followed by three readings from the Old Testament called *paremias*.

8. The Augmented Litany.

9. The prayer "Vouchsafe, O Lord" — recited.

10. The Litany of Supplication.

---

have mercy," but the remaining ones are answered with "Grant it, O Lord." Musically the litanies represent a point of repose (with the exception of the Augmented Litany, which has a heightened character) as well as a connecting link between different hymns.

On feast days, the Litiia is inserted at this point, consisting of (a) the Litiia stichera, sung by both choirs during the procession to the rear of the church, possibly in canonarchal style; (b) the prayer "O Lord, save Thy people," intoned by the deacon in five sections, answered each time by the choir singing "Lord, have mercy," repeated forty times, thirty times, fifty times, twice, and three times, respectively; (c) the return of the procession into the main part of the church; and (d) the closing prayer of the priest.

11. The stichera aposticha with inserted psalm verses —performed by both choirs in canonarchal style or antiphonally.

12. The Song of Simeon (*Nunc dimittis*)—usually sung.

12. The Song of Simeon—recited.

13. Trisagion and Lord's Prayer—recited.

14. The troparion of the day or feast—sung.

If a Litiia has been held, the five loaves of bread, grains of wheat, oil, and wine are blessed at this point, followed by the singing of Psalm 33.

15. The Augmented Litany (same as No. 8 in Great Vespers).

16. Benediction and dismissal.

If Great Vespers is part of an All-Night Vigil, Matins begins

directly following the benediction with the Six Psalms
(see outline of Matins).

For every service having a large number of sung hymns (Vespers, Matins, Divine Liturgy) there can be perceived a musical tension curve. The character of this curve may change for the same office depending on the solemnity of the occasion being celebrated on the particular day. The curve is determined by the styles of performance and the musical organization of the service—including melodic types and complexity of polyphonic settings—as well as such external factors as the movements of the clergy, the incensing of the church, processions, and the nature and degree of symbolism in the service.

Little Vespers has a much lower liturgico-musical tension curve, with fewer high points. The outline is as follows:

Little Vespers

1. Psalm 103—recited.
2. Vespers Psalms (same as No. 5 of Daily and Great Vespers) with four stichera of the day—sung.
3. Evening Hymn, "O Gladsome Light" — recited.
4. Prokeimenon of the day.
5. The prayer, "Vouchsafe, O Lord"—recited.
6. Stichera aposticha — sung.
7. The Song of Simeon—sung or recited.
8. The Trisagion and the Lord's Prayer—recited.
9. Troparion of the day—sung.
10. Abbreviated form of the Augmented Litany. (three petitions only).
11. Dismissal.

Matins

The second major service in the daily liturgical cycle that has a richness of sung hymnographical material is Matins. Three major varieties of Matins are outlined below, followed by the outlines of three entirely special forms of Matins—those of Great and Holy Friday, Great and Holy Saturday, and Easter.

Daily Matins

a) Without the Great Doxology (i.e., the Great Doxology is not sung, but recited):

b) With the Great Doxology (the Great Doxology is sung):

1. Following the opening benediction and prayers, Psalms 19 and 20 are recited, followed by the troparion and kontakion of the Cross, and a brief litany with a threefold "Lord, have mercy." Thereafter, Matins proper begins.

2. The Six Psalms (шестопсалмие)—3, 37, 62, 87, 102, and 142—recited.

3. The Great Litany.

4. The verse "God is the Lord . . ." and the troparion of the day with its corresponding theotokion—sung.

5. Two or three kathismas of the Psalter (according to the day and time of the year)—recited.

After each kathisma, the sedalen of the day—sung.

After each kathisma, a Little Litany, and the sedalen of the day—sung.

6. Psalm 50—recited.

7. Prayer of the deacon "O Lord, save Thy people," answered by "Lord, have mercy," sung twelve times.

8. The kanon: Odes 1 and 3, with the heirmoi sung and the troparia recited.

9. Little Litany, followed by the sedalen (or the kontakion of the lesser feast, if two commemorations fall on the same day).

10. Kanon: Odes 4, 5, and 6.

11. Little Litany, followed by the kontakion and oikos of the day.

12. Kanon: Odes 7 and 8.

13. Magnificat [15]—sung antiphonally, closing with Ode 9 of the kanon and the Marian hymn "It is truly meet," sung by both choirs joined together. Then a Little Litany.

14. Exaposteilarion — possibly sung, but usually recited.

15. The Psalms of Praise—148, 149, and 150—sometimes with interpolated stichera—sung or recited. The psalm group begins with the words "Praise the Lord from the heavens."

15. The Psalms of Praise—148, 149, and 150—always with interpolated stichera—always sung. The psalm group begins with the words "Let everything that breathes praise the Lord."

16. Following the psalms (or stichera, if present) the reader intones: "To Thee belongeth glory . . ." and then recites the Great Doxology *without the closing Trisagion.*

16. Following the final sticheron the Great Doxology is sung, *with the Trisagion,* and is followed by the troparion of the day and its closing theotokion, also sung.

17. Litany of Supplication.

17. Augmented Litany.

18. Stichera aposticha — sung in canonarchal style.

19. Trisagion and Lord's Prayer—recited.

20. Troparion of the day with its corresponding theotokion—sung.

21. Augmented Litany.

21. Litany of Supplication.

---

[15] Also referred to as честнѣйшую in Russian terminology, after the initial words of the refrain, "честнѣйшую херувимъ," sung after each verse of the Gospel text.

22. Closing dialogue between the priest and the choir
(or congregation), followed by the dismissal.

The end of Matins proper is followed directly by the First Hour,
which closes with the kontakion "O victorious leader."

Festal Matins

a) on Sundays: b) on Great Feasts:

1. The beginning is the same as that of Daily Matins.
If, however, Matins is celebrated as part of an All-
Night Vigil, this beginning is omitted, and Matins
begins immediately after the dismissal of Vespers with
the Six Psalms.

2. The Six Psalms—recited.

3. The Great Litany.

4. The verse "God is the Lord," followed by:

the resurrectional troparion   the troparion of the feast.
of the given Sunday, the tro-
parion to the saint(s) of the
day, and the theotokion.

5. Two or three kathismas of the Psalter—recited; following each kathisma, a Little Litany and a sedalen—
sung.

6. Either the Polyeleos (Psalms   6. The Polyeleos—sung in a
134 and 135) with the refrain   festive antiphonal manner.
"Alleluia" – sung,[16] or Psalm
118.

7. The five resurrectional tro-   7. The Magnification with
paria with the refrain "Blessed   refrains consisting of selected
art Thou, O Lord" (verse 12   verses from various psalms—
of Psalm 118)—sung.   sung in a festive antiphonal

[16] The Polyeleos is not prescribed for every Sunday of the year.

style. If a Marian feast or a feast of a saint coincides with a Sunday, the five resurrectional troparia are sung following the Magnification.

8. Little Litany, followed by:

the hypakoe of the tone governing the given Sunday and the sedalen after the Polyeleos—sung.

the sedalen or hypakoe of the feast—sung.

9. Three gradual antiphons of the tone governing the given Sunday—sung in antiphonal style.

9. The First Antiphon of the Fourth Tone, "From my youth"—sung.

10. The Sunday prokeimenon of the governing tone—sung in antiphonal-responsorial style.

10. The prokeimenon of the feast—sung in antiphonal-responsorial style.

11. One of the eleven Resurrection Gospel readings.

11. Gospel reading of the feast.

12. Hymn of the Resurrection "Having beheld the Resurrection of Christ"—sung; Psalm 50—recited; two short resurrectional stichera—sung.

12. Stichera of the feast—sung; Psalm 50—recited; stichera of feast—sung.

13. The prayer "O Lord, save Thy people," followed by a twelve-fold "Lord, have mercy."

14. Kanon: Odes 1 and 3; Little Litany.

15. The Sunday sedalen of the governing tone—sung.

15. The sedalen of the feast—sung.

16. Kanon: Odes 4, 5, and 6; Little Litany.

17. The Sunday kontakion and oikos of the governing tone—sung.

17. The kontakion and oikos of the feast—sung.

18. Kanon: Odes 7 and 8.

19. Magnificat — sung antiphonally.

19. On Great Feasts of the Lord and the Mother of God, special hypophons (refrains) to the stanzas of the Ninth Ode of the kanon; otherwise, the Magnificat.

20. Kanon: Ode 9; Little Litany.

21. One of the eleven exaposteilaria corresponding to the Gospel read earlier in the service.

21. The exaposteilarion of the feast.

22. The Psalms of Praise—148, 149, and 150—in the governing tone, with the Sunday stichera and, possibly, stichera to the saints of the day—sung antiphonally with a canonarch. The penultimate stanza is one of the eleven Matins Gospel stichera, while the last stanza is the theotokion "You are most blessed, O Virgin Theotokos."

22. The Psalms of Praise, with the stichera of the feast—sung by both choirs with a canonarch, in the tone of the first sticheron.

23. The Great Doxology with the Trisagion—sung either antiphonally or by both choirs joined in the middle of the church.

24. On Sundays governed by tones 1, 3, 5, 7, the resurrectional troparion "Today salvation has come"; on Sundays governed by tones 2, 4, 6, and 8, the resurrectional troparion

24. The troparion of the feast —sung.

"By rising from the tomb"—
both sung.

25. Augmented Litany.

26. Litany of Supplication.

27. Closing dialogue between the priest and choir; dismissal.

28. Following the dismissal, the First Hour.

The liturgico-musical tension curve of Daily Matins has very few pronounced high points. One might single out, in type *a*, Nos. 4 (the verse "God is the Lord" and the troparion) and 13 (the Magnificat), and in type *b*, Nos. 15 and 16 (Psalms 148-150 with stichera and the Great Doxology), in addition to Nos. 4 and 13, as relative high points.

By contrast, in Festal Matins there are many more peaks in the musical tension curve: Nos. 4 ("God is the Lord" and the troparion), 6-12 (from the Polyeleos through the festal stichera), 19 (the Ninth Ode of the kanon with refrains), and 21-23 (Psalms 148-150, with stichera, the Great Doxology, and the troparion of the feast). The intensity of the musical tension may vary with the character of a feast, and at times the high points in the tension curve may become rearranged, but essentially the scheme remains stable. The attention of the listener, however, is always held at various levels of tension through the vacillations in the intensity of the liturgico-musical element and through contrasts in the way that element is employed.

Especially varied from a musical standpoint are those sections of Vespers and Matins in which the hymns for the day of the week are juxtaposed with the hymns for the day of the year (e.g., the Sunday hymns in a given tone and the hymns in honor of a saint commemorated on that particular day of the year). These hymns consist primarily of stichera-groups and kanons, for which there may be prescribed melodies of different tones.[17]

---

[17] To take a representative example, at Vespers on a given Saturday evening that also happens to be the final day of the post-feast of a Marian feast and on which falls a commemoration of a saint, the following combination of stichera would occur on "Lord, I call upon Thee": four Sunday stichera in the governing tone of the week; three stichera of the Marian feast, possibly in another tone; three stichera of the saint, possibly in still another tone; on "Glory . . ."—the sticheron that would normally be sung at this point for the Marian feast, possibly in yet a different tone than any of the preceding

The rules governing the performance of kanons at Matins are particularly complex. As was stated in the preceding chapter, the basis for the kanon-poem is the nine Old Testament canticles, with newly-composed poetic material inserted within them. Thus, following a specified verse of a given Old Testament canticle, the heirmos of the corresponding ode of the kanon is sung. Then, following each subsequent Old Testament verse, a troparion of the corresponding ode. An ode may have fourteen, eight, six, or four Old Testament verses, and correspondingly, a large number of newly-composed stanzas (which may, however, be repeated, if necessary to correspond to the number of Old Testament verses).[18] In some cases the order of the day may prescribe a combination of several kanons (e.g., for Sunday, as well as for the commemoration of one or several saints), each of which may be performed in a different tone.[19]

From the usual format of Matins three important variants may be distinguished: the Matins of Great and Holy Friday,[20] Great and Holy Saturday,[21] and Easter, the last of which is celebrated on Easter night as well as every day of Easter week with only slight changes. The order and the character of these services differ from the customary format of Matins discussed above: the Matins of Great Friday and Great Saturday have a particularly pronounced dramatic character, in which the symbolic aspect of the liturgical action is greatly emphasized. The hymns, therefore, reflect the meaning of the symbolism.[22]

stichera; in closing, following "Both now and ever. . . ," the sticheron dogmatikon of the governing tone of the week (see, e.g., Typikon, p. 139v: combination for a Sunday on November 25). Thus, within a single group of stichera the tone may change five times! The same may hold true for other groups of stichera.

[18] In present-day practice, the Old Testament verses are employed only on the weekdays of Great Lent.

[19] See Chap. I.

[20] Celebrated in the evening of Great Thursday, ("In the second hour of the night," or approximately at 8:00 p.m., according to the Typikon, p. 449r). The Typikon reckons the hours from the moment of the setting of the sun, for the night, and from the moment of sunrise for the day.

[21] "In the seventh hour of the night," or approximately at 1:00 a.m. (Typikon, p. 454r).

[22] Orthodox liturgical ceremonies in general are replete with symbolic actions. In certain instances, the officiating bishop, for example, symbolizes Christ by his actions—not as an actor, but by creating a focal point for the worshippers' thoughts about Him. Similarly, the entrance of the clergy with the bread and wine during the Divine Liturgy is not a theatrical re-staging of Christ's festive entrance into Jerusalem on Palm Sunday; rather the liturgical action (i.e., the entrance) and the subsequent offering are symbolically associated with the historical entry into Jerusalem in the minds of the faithful. It

The order of worship for Great Friday and Great Saturday Matins originated from the passion services first held in Jerusalem. Originally, various parts of these Matins were celebrated at the locations in Jerusalem where the events of the passion, as described in the twelve Gospel readings of Great Friday, took place. The beginning of Great Friday Matins is the same as that of Daily Matins; for the purpose of comparison, however, the entire outline of the service is given below (cf. the outline on p. 78ff):

Matins of Great and Holy Friday

1. After the usual beginning—the Six Psalms; Great Litany.

2. In place of "God is the Lord," the refrain "Alleluia," sung to a special melody [23] alternately by both choirs, followed by the troparion, also alternately; Little Litany.

3. The first Gospel reading.

4. The First Antiphon (each stanza preceded by a verse) sung twice, once by each choir (in the eighth tone), followed directly by the Second Antiphon (in the sixth tone) and the Third Antiphon (in the second tone); Little Litany.

5. The sedalen (in the seventh tone), during which the congregation *stands*, however, while the priest censes the Sanctuary.

6. The second Gospel reading.

7. Three more antiphons (in the fifth, sixth, and seventh tones, respectively); Little Litany.

8. Sedalen in the seventh tone.

9. The third Gospel reading; each of the first five Gospel readings is followed by the same pattern: three antiphons—

is assumed, of course, that those attending the service have an understanding of the symbolic language employed.

[23] "Поемъ Аллилуіа . . .косно и со сладкопѣніемъ"—"We sing Alleluia slowly and melodically" (Typikon, p. 449r).

Little Litany—sedalen, until all fifteen antiphons are performed. After the fifth sedalen:

10. The sixth Gospel reading.

11. The Beatitudes (Matt. 5:1-12); after the fourth verse special stichera (in the fourth tone) are inserted between the verses of the Sermon on the Mount—sung alternately by both choirs; Little Litany.

12. Prokeimenon.

13. The seventh Gospel reading.

14. Psalm 50—recited.

15. The eighth Gospel reading.

16. The triodion of Great Friday (in the sixth tone), beginning with the fifth ode; the heirmos is repeated twice, while each of the two troparia—six times. At the end of the ode, the heirmos is repeated as a katabasia; [24] Little Litany.

17. The kontakion and oikos — sometimes sung.

18. Continuation of the triodion: odes 8 and 9 (the latter without the Magnificat), each with four troparia; Little Litany.

19. Exaposteilarion—sung thrice.

20. The ninth Gospel reading.

21. Psalms 148, 149, and 150 (in the third tone)—sung as in Festal Matins, with six interpolated stichera.

22. The tenth Gospel reading.

23. The Great Doxology — recited as in Daily Matins of type *a*.

---

[24] In this case, the Triodion consists of Odes 5, 8, and 9.

24. The Litany of Supplication.

25. The eleventh Gospel reading.

26. Six stichera aposticha—sung in canonarchal style.

27. The twelfth Gospel reading.

28. Trisagion and Lord's Prayer—recited.

29. A special troparion in the fourth tone—sung.

30. The Augmented Litany.

31. Closing dialogue and dismissal. (The First Hour is not read.[25])

As can be seen from this outline, this service is extraordinarily rich in sung hymns: fifteen antiphons, six sedalens, three odes of the triodion, two groups of stichera, the stichera on the Beatitudes, etc.,—this in addition to the usual responses. However, while the twelve Gospel readings and the numerous hymns sung in various tones and styles lend an extremely solemn character to the service, augmented by the lighted candles held by the worshippers, the Great Doxology at the end of the service is not sung, but recited.

Another special case is presented by the Matins of Great and Holy Saturday, which begins in a somber and solemn mood, but ends joyfully and festively.

Matins of Great and Holy Saturday

1. The beginning, through the verse "God is the Lord" and the troparion, is the same as for Daily Matins. The deviations from the usual format begin following the troparion.

2. Immediately after the troparion, kathisma 17 of the Psalter, Psalm 118, is performed in three sections or stases (статьи). Each verse of the psalm is followed by a special

---

[25] No Divine Liturgy (including the Liturgy of Presanctified Gifts) is celebrated on Great Friday; thus, no communion is offered.

stanza, called a "eulogy" or "praise" (μεγαλυνάριον; похвала) in praise of the buried Christ; the psalm verses are sung by the choir, while the praises are chanted by the priests from the middle of the church. The melodies of the first two stases are both in the fifth tone, but of different melodic construction. The third stasis suddenly changes to the festive mood of the third tone. Between the first and second stases there is a Little Litany. Following the third stasis, the five resurrectional troparia (see No. 5 of Sunday Matins) are sung, followed by a Little Litany.

3. The rest of the service essentially follows the usual format of Daily Matins with the Great Doxology, except that the Magnificat is not sung before the Ninth Ode of the kanon.

4. As the Trisagion at the end of the Great Doxology is reached, the procession around the church with the Shroud (ἐπιτάφιον; плащаница) forms and proceeds out of the church building. During the procession, the final trisagion is sung to a slow, extended melody.

5. Following the return into the church, the troparion of Great Saturday is sung.

6. Prokeimenon, followed by the reading from Ezekiel 37.

7. Second prokeimenon, followed by the epistle reading.

8. Alleluia with verses (as during Divine Liturgy), followed by the Gospel reading.

9. Litanies and conclusion the same as in Sunday Matins.

The most conspicuous feature of this service is the manner in which kathisma 17 with the interpolated stanzas is performed, resulting in the constantly rising intensity of the musical tension curve: the service begins with the somber fifth tone, becoming somewhat more joyful during the second stasis, and still brighter during the third stasis sung in the festive third tone. The first high point is reached with the resurrectional troparia, while the second high point occurs during the Great Doxology, especially in the solemn trisagion during the procession. The heightened mood continues then through the Scripture readings and to the conclusion of the service.

The Matins of Easter

The Matins service of Easter has an entirely special format and musical tension curve, which bear only a general resemblance to the structure of ordinary Matins. Easter Matins (Russian: заутреня, i.e., "a service before the dawn") begins with a procession around the church,[26] during which one of the Sunday stichera (from the aposticha in the sixth tone) is sung. The actual beginning of the service takes place outside of the church in front of the closed entrance doors.

1. After the opening benediction, the clergy sing the troparion of Easter, "Christ is risen," three times, which is then repeated by the choir and congregation. The priest then sings four verses from Psalm 67 ("Let God arise . . ."), each verse being answered by the Easter troparion. In conclusion the priest sings the first half of the troparion, while the choir answers with the second half. The priest then knocks with the hand-cross upon the church doors, which are opened from inside. The procession enters the church to the singing of the troparion.

2. The Great Litany.

3. The Easter kanon (both heirmoi and troparia) is sung alternately by both choirs, with the final heirmos of each ode sung by both choirs joined together. After each closing heirmos (katabasia), the Easter troparion is repeated three times, followed by a Little Litany.

4. The entire kanon is performed in this manner, with each ode followed by a Little Litany (not each group of odes, as in the usual case). In place of the Magnificat there are short laudatory refrains (hypophons) sung to the stanzas of the ninth ode.[27] After the third ode — the hypakoe; after the sixth ode — the kontakion and oikos,

---

[26] Symbolizing the journey of the myrrhbearing women to the tomb of Christ. In Greek, Bulgarian and Serbian practice, the Gospel account of that journey is read in front of the church doors, before the beginning of the actual Easter Matins service.

[27] The distinguishing feature of the Easter services is that, except for the prayers and ekphonesis of the priests, nothing is recited or psalmodized: everything is sung.

followed by the resurrectional hymn, "Having beheld the Resurrection of Christ" (see No. 12 of Sunday Matins) and the resurrectional sticheron, repeated three times.

5. Exaposteilarion (in the third tone).

6. The Psalms of Praise (148, 149, and 150), with the four Sunday stichera of the first tone—sung alternately by both choirs in canonarchal style.

7. The five festive Paschal stichera—sung by both choirs joined in the middle of the church, closing with a manifold repetition of the Easter troparion.

8. Solemn reading (in ordinary speaking voice) of the Easter Homily of St. John Chrysostom. The reading is concluded with the singing of the troparion in praise of St. John.

9. Litanies as in Festal Matins.

10. Following the closing dialogue the Easter troparion is sung several times, and following the dismissal—a special closing verse, "And unto us He has given eternal life . . ."

The focal point of Easter Matins is the kanon: the entire section of Matins that usually precedes the kanon is omitted in this instance. For this reason the shape of the musical tension curve is different than in any other service: it does not gradually build or increase in tension, but begins at the highest point. Viewed from a purely musical standpoint the kanon is uncomplicated, consisting of one or two melodic phrases constantly repeated. The tension is maintained, however, by other means: the continuous incensing of the church by the priests, the lighted candles held by all those present, the uninterrupted exchanges between the choirs, etc. Following the kanon the tension curve drops: the peaceful, melodic character of the exaposteilarion provides a point of relaxation. After that, however, the tension curve rises once again during the Psalms of Praise, the resurrectional stichera and the paschal stichera. This part of the service is, nevertheless, more peaceful and not as impulsive as the first. Were this section connected directly to the kanon without a point of relaxation in between, a certain feeling of fatigue would be experienced, instead of a second high point.

Divine Liturgy

Whereas Vespers and Matins are particularly rich in constantly changing propers displaying a great variety of musical forms and styles, the Divine Liturgy contains comparatively few changeable propers. Consisting for the most part of ordinaries, the structure of the Divine Liturgy remains very constant. The few propers that occur are found primarily in the first part of the service, the "Liturgy of the Catechumens."

Much has been written about the Divine Liturgy, and its structure is generally better known than those of Vespers and Matins. Nevertheless it is worthwhile to examine the format of the Liturgy with particular regard to its musical organization.

The Orthodox Church employs three forms of the Divine Liturgy: (1) the Liturgy of St. John Chrysostom, (2) the Liturgy of St. Basil the Great, and (3) the Liturgy of the Presanctified Gifts. The difference between the first two is found primarily in the quiet prayers of the priest, which are considerably longer in the Liturgy of St. Basil. For this reason the hymns sung during the quiet prayers of that Liturgy, while having identical texts with the Liturgy of St. John, must be sung to more elaborate and melismatic melodies in order to cover the duration of the prayers. These differences are present only in the "Liturgy of the Faithful" (which begins with the first Litany of the Faithful); the first parts of both liturgies are identical.[28]

The basic structure of the Divine Liturgy is the same on all occasions, on major feasts as well as ordinary weekdays. The only difference lies in the character and degree of festiveness displayed in the hymn settings.

Divine Liturgy

A. Liturgy of the Catechumens (Liturgy of the Word):

1. Opening benediction and Great Litany.

2. The First Antiphon from the psalms (varies with the

[28] The Liturgy of St. Basil is celebrated only ten times during the year: (1) on the Eve of the Nativity; (2) on the Eve of Theophany; (3) on January 1 (the feast of St. Basil); (4-8) on the Sundays of Great Lent, with the exception of Palm Sunday; (9) on Great Thursday; and (10) on Great Saturday.

feast day)—sung antiphonally, possibly with a hypophon; Little Litany.

3. The Second Antiphon—sung in the same manner as the first, but ending always with the troparion "Only-begotten Son"; Little Litany.

4. The Third Antiphon—sung like the first and second. During the singing of this antiphon the Little Entrance of the clergy with Gospel takes place, followed by the introit verse (varies according to the feast).

5. Troparia and kontakia of the day (may be several, depending on the occasion)—sung in various tones by both choirs in alternation.

6. The Trisagion—sung alternately by both choirs, and, occasionally, by the clergy as well.

7. Prokeimenon of the epistle reading—sung antiphonally-responsorially in the prescribed tone.

8. Epistle reading of the day.

9. Alleluia with psalm verses—sung antiphonally-responsorially in the prescribed tone for the day or feast.

10. The Gospel reading of the day.[29]

11. The Augmented Litany.

12. The Litany of the Catechumens.

B. Liturgy of the Faithful:

13. The first and second Litanies of the Faithful.

14. The Cherubic Hymn (χερουβικόν; херувимская

---

[29] The sermon is generally given during the Divine Liturgy either following the Gospel reading; during the communion of the clergy, by one of the non-celebrating priests; or shortly before the dismissal. During festal Matins, usually after the Gospel reading, directly before the kanon. At private offices, before the beginning.

пѣснь)—sung in a solemn manner, occasionally by both choirs joined in the middle of the church. During the Cherubic Hymn, the Great Entrance of the clergy with the bread and wine for the Eucharist takes place.[30]

15. The first Litany of Supplication.

16. The Creed—recited or sung by the congregation and/or the choir.

17. The Eucharistic Canon (Anaphora), which consists of (a) a dialogue between the priest and choir ("A mercy of peace . . ."), (b) the Hymn of Praise ("It is meet and right to worship . . ."), (c) the Sanctus ("Holy, holy, holy . . ."), (d) the words of Christ "Take, eat, this is my body . . ." and "Drink of it, all of you, this is my blood . . . ," ekphonated by the priest, and (e) the Hymn of Thanksgiving ("We praise Thee . . ."); the Anaphora is sometimes sung by both choirs joined together.

18. The Hymn to the Theotokos,—often sung by both choirs joined together. This hymn changes with the feast: the Liturgy of St. Basil has its own special hymn, while on feast days of the Lord and the Mother of God, the ninth ode of the kanon, with the refrain, is usually sung.

19. The second Litany of Supplication.

20. The Lord's Prayer—recited or sung by the congregation and/or the choir.

21. The Communion Hymn (a proper of the day)—sung during the communion of the clergy in the Sanctuary. On occasions when there are many priests concelebrating, and the communion of the clergy takes longer than usual, another hymn that is appropriate for the day may

[30] Although the Cherubic Hymn, "Иже херувимы," is one of the stable hymns of the ordinary for Divine Liturgy, on Great Thursday and Great Saturday a different text is sung in its place than on every other day of the year. In the tenth-twelfth centuries, however, other texts were substituted much more frequently. Thus, strictly speaking, one must conclude that the usual text of the Cherubic Hymn belongs to the ordinary only provisionally.

be sung in addition to the specified Communion Hymn.

22. The appearance of the Holy Gifts and the communion of the faithful, during which the communion
verse "Receive the Body of Christ . . ." is sung.

23. Prayers and hymns of thanksgiving; Litany of
Thanksgiving; closing prayer, benediction, and dismissal.

As can be seen from the outline above, the changing propers
are contained almost entirely in the Liturgy of the Catechumens.
The invariable hymns (ordinaries) have no tones or special melodies
prescribed for them, a circumstance that gives the performers a
certain degree of freedom in their choice of musical setting. The
shape of the liturgico-musical tension curve in the Divine Liturgy
is wave-like: it rises for the first time towards the Little Entrance and
then again at the Augmented Litany. After that it sinks somewhat,
rising again at the Cherubic Hymn. Following another brief release
(Nos. 15 and 16), it builds continually towards another high point
at the Hymn of Thanksgiving during the Anaphora, then falls, following the Hymn to the Theotokos. The course and outline of the
tension curve may, of course, change on specific occasions, such as
various feasts. Also, a Pontifical Liturgy (a Liturgy in which a bishop
is the chief celebrant) has its own special character and high points.

The outline of the Divine Liturgy presented above changes on
a few special occasions, and then, only in the first part of the service:
thus, on the eves of the Nativity and the Theophany, on Annunciation
and on Great Thursday and Great Saturday, the first part of the
Liturgy is replaced by Vespers, whereby the Vespers/Liturgy unit
becomes related to the events of the next calendar day. The transition
from Vespers to the Liturgy proper takes place following the last
reading (*paremia*) from the Old Testament (see outline of Great
Vespers, note after No. 7), which is followed by a Little Litany and
the Trisagion (No. 6 in the outline of the Divine Liturgy), and then
the remainder of the Divine Liturgy (in these cases, that of St. Basil).

The Liturgy of the Presanctified Gifts contains no Eucharistic
Canon or consecration of the Gifts, and consists essentially of Vespers
closing with communion, for which the Holy Gifts had been con-
secrated during the last Liturgy of St. John or St. Basil. This Liturgy
is performed on Wednesdays and Fridays of the first six weeks
of Great Lent and on Monday, Tuesday and Wednesday of Holy
Week. The outline is as follows:

The Liturgy of the Presanctified Gifts

1. The service begins with Daily Vespers as usual, except that the kathisma of the Psalter (No. 3 in the outline of Vespers) is almost always kathisma 8, psalmodized in three sections with a Little Litany after each section.

2. The Vesper Psalms (No. 5 in the outline of Vespers) always have ten stichera interpolated among them.

3. Following the Evening Hymn, "O Gladsome Light," and the entrance of the clergy into the Sanctuary, the first prokeimenon and the first Old Testament reading; then another prokeimenon and the second Old Testament reading. Following these readings, the Liturgy proper begins.

4. The hymn "Let my prayer arise," consisting of four verses from Psalm 140, each followed by a refrain—usually performed by a solo singer (or a trio) in the middle of the church with the refrains sung by the choir.

5. The Prayer of St. Ephraim the Syrian—recited by the priest.

6. Augmented Litany; Litany of the Catechumens; two Litanies of the Faithful (different from those in the Liturgy of St. John).

7. The hymn "Now the powers of heaven," during which the Presanctified Gifts are transferred in solemn procession from the Table of Oblation to the Altar Table. This hymn replaces the Cherubic Hymn of the Liturgies of St. John and St. Basil; then the Prayer of St. Ephraim.

8. Litany of Supplication.

9. The Lord's Prayer—sung.

10. The Communion Hymn during the communion of the clergy.

11. The communion of the faithful. The remainder of the

service follows the same format as the Liturgies of St. John and St. Basil, but with slightly different texts and melodies.

Thus, in the Liturgy of Presanctified Gifts, the most solemn part (from the Creed to the Hymn to the Mother of God) is omitted. The musical high points are the hymn "Let my prayer arise," sung while the congregation kneels, and the hymn "Now the powers of heaven."

The Royal Hours

One other special order of service is found on the eves of the Nativity and the Theophany, and on Great Friday, when the First, Third, Sixth, and Ninth Hours are combined consecutively to form the so-called *Royal Hours* (царские часы).[31] The format is the same as that of ordinary Hours, but with several additional parts (marked here by +) added to each of the Hours. The outline is as follows:

The Royal Hours

1. After the opening prayers, three psalms (which change according to the feast)—recited.

2. The troparion of the feast or a special troparion with a theotokion; then, another special troparion, sung alternately by both choirs (+).

3. Prokeimenon — sung antiphonally-responsorially (+).

4. Reading from the Old Testament; epistle reading; Gospel reading (+).

5. The Trisagion and the Lord's Prayer—recited.

6. Kontakion of the day.

7. Closing prayer of the respective Hour.

8. In cathedrals when a bishop is present, following the

[31] So called because in earlier times this festive service was traditionally attended by the Tsar or Emperor.

entire group of Hours, the Many Years (многолетие), including the full title of the ruler, is intoned by the proto-deacon and answered by the singers [32] (+).

Other Offices

In the discussion above, only those offices in which singing plays an important role have been considered. The remaining offices, such as Compline and Nocturn, do not contain a significant amount of sung material except during Great Lent, Holy Week, and Easter Week. Whether sung or not, the hymns in these offices are the same as those found in the Vespers and Matins of the day, and are performed in the same fashion.

Two other offices that are almost entirely sung may be celebrated either in the church building or elsewhere, in which case they take on the character of private services: (1) The Prayer Service of petition, praise, or thanksgiving (молебен; молебное пение), and (2) the Memorial Service (παραστάς; панихида). In their structure both services are essentially an abridged form of Matins. The Prayer Service consists of a troparion, a kanon (abbreviated), a prokeimenon, and a Gospel reading (no Great Doxology). The Memorial Service has virtually the same structure, but no Gospel reading, and contains some additional stichera towards the end. The Prayer Service is sometimes held during a procession around the church.

The only other offices remaining to be considered are those that do not belong to the weekly, yearly or Triodion cycles, but, like the Prayer and Memorial Services, are performed as the need arises. To this category belong such offices as the Consecration of a Bishop, the Ordination of Priests and Deacons, the Dedication of a Church Building, the Rite of Holy Matrimony, the Rite of Burial, the Blessing of the Waters, all of which are, to a large extent, sung. The hymns contained in these offices do not, however, add anything new or different to the system of Russian Orthodox liturgical singing, since in all cases they belong to one of the hymnographical forms found in other offices—troparia, prokeimena, stichera, etc. For this reason these hymns are of greater interest to the liturgiologist than to the church musician.

The outlines of the various services presented above cannot satisfactorily relate one very important factor that has a significant

---

[32] The Many Years (without the title of the ruler) may also be sung at the close of the Divine Liturgy or private offices, using texts that are appropriate to the occasion.

influence upon the musical organization of Orthodox worship: the visual aspect of the liturgical actions that take place during the singing of various hymns (e.g., the solemn entrances of the clergy into the Sanctuary, the blessings by the priest, the incensing of the church, the various degrees of illumination in the church prescribed in the Typikon, etc.). The details of these actions will have to be discussed elsewhere. It can only be pointed out here that the entire environment, including such factors as the deportment of the faithful at worship, the visual appearance of the icons and frescoes as well as the liturgical actions of the clergy, influences the manner in which the musical element is employed in the liturgy. Thus a unified whole is formed, in which all elements are dependent upon one another, being also influenced by the national religious temperament of the people in whose midst these factors develop.

CHAPTER III

The System of Russian Liturgical Singing

Canonical and Non-Canonical Singing

As was mentioned earlier, each national branch of the Orthodox Church has its own particular type of liturgical singing that is the result of a slow but continual development of liturgico-musical forms. Thus, it is possible to identify individual systems of liturgical singing for each respective national branch. The development of a given system is influenced by the musical aptitude and feeling of the particular nationality, the peculiarities of the liturgical language,[1] and the history of the nation and its church. All of the above factors served to distinguish the system of liturgical singing in the Russian Orthodox Church from those of other Orthodox churches, especially non-Slavic ones. At no time has this difference been more marked than in the present day.

From the start, it is necessary to distinguish two major categories of liturgical singing: (1) The liturgical singing of the official ruling church—the State Church of Russia—i.e., that part of the Russian Orthodox Church that accepted the reforms in liturgical practice carried out by Patriarch Nikon in the middle of the seventeenth century; and (2) the liturgical singing of the so-called Old Believers (староверы or старообрядцы), a group of Orthodox who did not accept the reforms of Patriarch Nikon and formed two distinct factions: those possessing a hierarchy separate from that of the official Church, and those with no hierarchy at all.[2] While the singing of the Old Believers is exclusively canonical (уставное пение), the singing of the official church includes both canonical and non-canonical singing (неуставное пение).[3]

The distinction between canonical and non-canonical singing applies only to the musical aspects of the liturgical singing, since all liturgical texts are by definition canonical; other texts cannot even be

---

[1] Concerning the correct pronunciation of the liturgical texts of the Russian Church, see. B. A. Uspenskii, Архаическая система церковно-славянского произношения (из истории литургического произношения в России) [The archaic system of Church Slavonic pronunciation (from the history of liturgical pronunciation in Russia)] (Moscow: Издание Московского Университета, 1968).

[2] The former are referred to as поповцы, the latter as безпоповцы.

[3] From уставъ — Typikon.

101

considered.[4] The term "canonical" refers to singing that consists of melodies contained in official liturgical singing-books—either ancient manuscripts written in staffless notation, or printed books with staff notation published by the Holy Synod of the Russian Church. It makes no difference whether these melodies are performed in unison—their original form—or in two, three, or four voices; as long as the original canonical melody is maintained, the singing may be termed canonical. By contrast, non-canonical singing consists of freely-composed polyphonic settings of liturgical texts, which, although intended for use in the liturgy, do not employ canonical melodies, and in various other ways do not fulfill the requirements placed upon liturgical singing by the Typikon.[5]

This is not to say that all polyphonic (non-unison) singing is non-canonical. The performance of canonical melodies in polyphonic settings became a standard practice in the Russian Church since the middle of the seventeenth century, and can, therefore, be considered an aspect of canonical singing. The early examples of such polyphony were largely improvised by doubling the main melody at the interval of a third, if there were only two voices singing; if there were three voices, the third voice provided a harmonic bass line suggested by the movement of the top two voices. A fourth voice, when present, filled in the missing chord tones. What resulted was not a free composition or an artistic harmonization, but an improvised polyphonic setting of the canonical melody.

Within the canonical liturgical singing of the Russian Orthodox Church it is possible to identify several different systems or *chants* (роспевы).[6] In this context, a chant is a system of melodies that

---

[4] Certain hymns or songs of a religious nature whose texts are not contained in liturgical service-books and, therefore, not intended for use in the liturgy, may be termed *paraliturgical singing* (see p. 111 below). Such hymns may be performed outside the context of church worship, but in certain instances are included in various services: a typical example is the "concert," "Come to me from Lebanon," sung for the meeting of the bride at a Wedding Service. The text, which is from the Song of Songs, is not found in any liturgical service book.

[5] In the Russian literature on the subject of liturgical singing the expressions уставное пение (canonical singing) and неуставное пение (non-canonical singing) are used rather frequently, but are not precisely defined. Canonical singing must be understood as singing that is prescribed by the Typikon (уставъ), both in terms of actual melodic material and the style of performance to be employed. It is canonical in the sense that it has been canonized and recognized by Church authorities to be correct and proper for use in the liturgy.

[6] *Translator's note:* The term роспев (pl.: роспевы, also расцев, распевы) will be subsequently translated as "chant." The author's definition of роспев corresponds to the concept of chant in Western music history.

have in common certain aesthetic principles, origins, and characteristic ways of correlating the musical material with texts of varying
syllabic structure. The systems of chants can be divided into two
categories: (1) *Complete chants* (полные роспевы), which contain
melodies for all groups and types of hymns mentioned in Chapter I;
and (2) *Incomplete chants* (неполные роспевы), which have melodies only for certain types of hymns, e.g., only for troparia and heirmoi, but none for stichera, etc.

Furthermore, within the framework of each chant there may
exist other sub-systems: (a) *Great chant* (большой роспев), the
melodies of which are characterized by richly developed melodic
forms, with frequently-occurring melismas of as many as four
distinct pitches over a single syllable of text; (b) *Middle chant*
(средний роспев), with less-developed melodies of a syllabic or
neumatic structure; and (c) *Little chant* (малый роспев), in which
recitative upon a single note prevails, with only occasional two- or
three-note melismas.[7]

Within the context of a given chant system (*rospev*), it is necessary to distinguish still another category: melodies for a given type
or group of hymns, often referred to as *napevy* (напевы; lit.: melodies, tunes) or in older terminology, *perevody* (переводы; lit.: translations, interpretations). Thus, in the sixteenth century, for example,
one finds references to *Lukoshkov perevod*—the interpretation of
Lukoshko. The term *napevy* refers either to a group of melodies
related to a specific hymnographical group (e.g., the *napevy* of
stichera within the system of Znamenny Chant), or, more commonly,
to melodic variants of local or regional origin (e.g., *Moskovskii
napev*—the Moscow melody or variant of a given chant, or *Valaamskii
napev*—the variant of the Valaam Monastery).[8] Often the origin of
the variant is not specified, but is simply designated in liturgical chant-
books as инъ роспѣвъ, i.e., a "different melody" within the framework of a given chant system.

Generally speaking, up to the end of the nineteenth century,
Russian literature on liturgical singing did not make careful distinctions between the use of the terms *rospev* and *napev*. Local variants
were often given the designation *rospev*, whereas, more properly,

---

[7] I. I. Voznesenskii, Большой и малый знаменный роспев [The Great and
Little Znamenny Chant] (Riga: 1890), p. 86; N. P. Potulov, Руководство к
практическому изучению древняго пения православной российской церкви
[A guide to the practical study of the ancient singing of the Orthodox Russian
Church], 3rd ed., (Moscow: 1898), p. 30, n. 2.

[8] The regional and local variants of canonical melodies (such as those
from various monasteries) are considered to be part of canonical singing.

they should have been termed *napev*. For this reason there is still considerable confusion regarding the proper use of these two terms.

The canonical singing of the Russian Church consists of four chant systems of primary importance and two others of secondary importance:

1. *Znamenny* or *Stolp Chant* (знаменный or столповой роспев): [9] This is the most ancient and most complete chant of the Russian Church. Its oldest written monuments date back to the end of the eleventh or beginning of the twelfth centuries, and its development can be observed throughout history until the eighteenth and nineteenth centuries. In the early manuscripts the melodies are notated by means of staffless neumes or signs, знамена (sign: знамя), from which the chant derives its name. Because of their physical appearance, the neumes were also called крюки, "hooks." The term знамя evidently referred not only to the individual musical signs, but also to notation in general.[10] Thus, the term *znamenny rospev* originally distinguished chant that was set down in some type of written notation from that which was passed along by oral tradition.

The other name for this chant system, Stolp Chant,[11] is derived from столп or pillar, the eight-week-long cycle of eight tones described earlier. In other words, Stolp Chant is a chant that follows the eight-tone system. Accordingly, the notation by means of which

---

[9] Special studies of znamenny (stolp) notation include: Johann v. Gardner and Erwin Koschmieder, *Ein handschriftliches Lehrbuch der altrussischen Neumenschrift*, Vol. I—Text (Munich: 1963); Vol. II—Kommentar zum Zeichensystem (Munich: 1966); Vol. III—Kommentar zum Tropensystem (Munich: 1972); S. Smolenskii, Азбука знаменнаго пѣнія (извѣщеніе о соглас-нѣйшихъ помѣтахъ старца Александра Мезенца (1668-го года) [The Alphabet of Znamenny Singing (information concerning the consonant marks) of the Elder, Aleksandr Mezenets (1668)] (Kazan: 1888); V. Metallov, Азбука крюкового пения [The alphabet of "hook" singing] (Moscow: 1899) and later editions: Oskar v. Riesemann, *Die Notationen des alt-russischen Kirchengesangs* (Leipzig: 1909).

[10] E.g., демественное знамя (demestvenny notation), путевое знамя (put' notation)—terms pertaining to the notations of other types of singing. Staff notation, which was brought to Muscovy by Kievan singers in the mid-seventeenth century, was also termed Киевское знамя (Kievan notation). See V. Metallov, Очеркъ исторіи православнаго церковнаго пения въ Россіи [Essay on the history of Orthodox church singing in Russia] (Moscow: 1900), p. 57.

[11] *Translator's note:* Since the term "Znamenny Chant" has come to be accepted in English usage, this translation will continue to use the term "znamenny," rather than "stolp," in reference to the chant itself. However, in referring to the actual notation of Znamenny Chant, it will be necessary on occasion to refer to столповое знамя (stolp notation), since there are other notations that employ the term знамя (see n. 10 above).

this chant is notated is referred to as столповое знамя or столповая нотация, "stolp notation." [12]

The system of Znamenny Chant contains melodies for all hymnographical groups of hymns: (1) stichera, (2) troparia, kontakia, and sedalens, (3) heirmoi of kanons, (4) prokeimena, alleluias, and other short responsorial hymns, and (5) certain unchanging (ordinary) hymns of Divine Liturgy and Vigil. The melodies are organized according to eight tones and include all three levels of melodic complexity—Great, Middle, and Little.

2. *Kievan Chant* (киевский роспев): [13] From an historical point of view Kievan Chant may be seen as a variety of Znamenny Chant that came into being at the time when the western and southwestern parts of the Russian metropolitanate (originally principalities under the founding dynasty of Rurik) were under the rule of Lithuanian and Polish kings. Kievan Chant is also based on a system of eight tones, and follows the same principles of melodic construction as the Znamenny. However, the evolution of Kievan Chant out of the original Znamenny did not occur without a certain influence from Western European music. Having developed as a regional variant, Kievan Chant gained in importance when it was brought to Moscow by church singers from Kiev at the invitation of Tsar Aleksei Mikhailovich and Patriarch Nikon, following the political union between eastern Ukraine and Muscovy in 1654. Although Kievan Chant is a complete chant, containing melodies for all hymnographical groups, it is not as rich and varied as the Znamenny in its melodic content.

3. *Greek Chant* (греческий роспев): [14] This chant is not complete, lacking melodies for certain categories of hymns, such as

---

[12] The interpretation of the word столп (στήλη or στῦλος—column, pillar, post) as "sign" or "neume" is erroneous, when applied to musical notation: while it is possible to interpret the term столповое пение as "neumatic singing," the same interpretation would make the oft-used expression столповое знамя a tautology. It is obvious, therefore, that the adjective столповое pertains not to the notational signs, but rather, to the type of singing that follows the eight-week Pillar of Tones. See Johann v. Gardner and Erwin Koschmieder, *op. cit.* Vol. II, p. 1; D. Razumovskii, Церковное пение в России [Church singing in Russia] Vol. 1 (Moscow: 1867) p. 121; V. Metallov, Очерк..., p. 57; V. Metallov, Азбука..., p. 2.

[13] Special treatise: I. I. Voznesenskii, Осмогласные роспевы трех последних веков православной русской церкви [Eight-tone chants of the three last centuries of the Russian Orthodox Church] Vol. 1: Киевский роспев [Kievan Chant] (Moscow: 1898).

[14] *Ibid.*, Vol. 3: Греческий роспев в России [Greek Chant in Russia] (Kiev: 1893).

stichera and prokeimena.[15] Although it is called "Greek," it has nothing in common with the liturgical singing of the Greeks—Byzantine Chant. On no account should it be confused with the Byzantine singing that was brought by the Greeks to Kievan Russia in the ninth-tenth centuries. Greek Chant is of much later origin, having been notated in the mid-seventeenth century by Ukrainian and Muscovite singing-masters from the singing of several Greek clerics and cantors known to have been in Moscow at the time. As they were being notated, the melodies were russified beyond recognition, partially due to the fact that the diatonic scale and the system of staff notation employed by the Russians were totally unsuited for transcribing the elaborate modality and unusual intervals of the Greek singing. The chants were written down primarily in staff notation and only partially in stolp notation.

It is also possible that some of the melodies of Greek Chant were written down in Kiev, where Greek singers were also known to have been. In any case, the melodies of Greek Chant included in the Synodal chant-books exhibit a close similarity in their structure to those of Kievan Chant—strophic-periodic form and characteristics of mensural and harmonic principles derived unquestionably from Western European music, with which singers in the Ukraine were already familiar due to close contacts with Poland and the music of the Roman Catholic Church.

Greek Chant is also based on the principle of eight tones.

4. *Bulgarian Chant* (болгарский роспев):[16] This chant, also containing melodies in eight tones, is incomplete, consisting of a relatively small number of melodies only for certain hymns. The chant, notated in square-note staff notation, was also brought to Muscovy by Ukrainian singers in the middle of the seventeenth century. Although it is called "Bulgarian," it is impossible to say definitely whether the chant is indeed of Bulgarian origin, due to the lack of thorough research into the history of church singing in Bulgaria. The present-day liturgical singing of the Bulgarians is quite different—late-Byzantine, adopted to the Church-Slavonic language with Bulgarian pronunciation—and bears no resemblance to the Bulgarian Chant of the Russian Church. Since no written monuments of Bulgarian singing contemporary with the Christianization of the Rus' have yet been discovered, the designation of this chant as "Bulgarian" must, for the time being, remain provisional.

[15] Only the melody for prokeimena in the fourth tone is known.
[16] I. I. Voznesenskii, Vol. 2: — Болгарский роспев [Bulgarian Chant] (Kiev: 1891).

The four chants described above are the most important ones in the system of present-day Russian canonical singing. In addition, there are two more types or systems of singing that must be viewed as canonical, but reserved for special festive occasions. In the sixteenth through eighteenth centuries these two systems occupied a prominent place in the scheme of Russian liturgical singing, but in the course of the eighteenth century they almost completely lost their significance, and only a few of their melodies were included in the Synodal singing-books (and only in some editions). These systems are (1) *Put' Chant* (путевой роспев or путное пение) and (2) *Demestvenny Singing* (демественное пение or демество). Both of these systems have been barely researched. In is known, however, that both have their own types of neumatic staffless notation derived from stolp (znamenny) notation.

Put' Chant in all probability represents a variety of Znamenny Chant. Its melodies are organized according to the eight tones, but are generally more melismatic than Znamenny melodies, frequently displaying a syncopated character. Overall, Put' Chant most closely resembles the Great Znamenny Chant.

The origin of the term путевой in reference to the chant is unclear. In antiquity, the word путь meant "method," "means," or "custom," in addition to the present-day meaning of "road" or "path." [17] Razumovskii, however, and other writers who uncritically accepted his conclusions, attempted to explain the term путевой роспев literally, as a type of singing used "on the road," i.e. outside of the church building:

> The origin of znamenny put' singing is related to the piety of our ancestors, who, not wishing to forego observing worship services during their frequent distant pilgrimages and travels, unfailingly served Divine Liturgy, Vespers, Matins, Nocturn, etc. At the same time, out of pious respect for the temple and its implements (vestments, church utensils, etc.), they did not dare to use the old eight-tone [stolp] chant while travelling on the road, since these things properly belonged to the temple and the choir. Thus, for singing during travel they composed a special chant, which followed the eight tones, that came to be called put' because of its use on the road. [18]

[17] I. I. Sreznevskii, Материалы для словаря древне-русского языка [Materials for a dictionary of the ancient Russian language], Vol. 2, ser. 2 (St. Petersburg: 1898), col. 1736-1740.
[18] D. Razumovskii, Богослужебное пение православной греко-российской

The artificiality of this explanation is evident even without detailed analysis. Razumovskii's statement is contradicted from the outset by the fact that Put' Chant was employed for the particularly festive hymns of Vespers and Matins, hymns sung during the consecration of a church building, and other occasions that specifically occurred within the context of worship *in the church building*. Moreover, the complex melodic construction of Put' melodies demands well-trained, experienced singers. By contrast, services performed while travelling are usually simplified in some fashion, and, due to the absence of a church building, are inevitably less solemn and festive than those performed inside a church. If, as Razumovskii suggests, Put' Chant was employed during pilgrimages, it is difficult to imagine that the pilgrims would not be able to find a single church in a village or monastery along the way. All these contradictions make Razumovskii's explanation extremely doubtful.

Another explanation is that the term путь must be understood as a *cantus firmus*, a voice to which the other voices must equate themselves in multi-voiced, non-unison performance.[19] In polyphonic (usually three-voiced) staffless scores of the sixteenth century (троестрочное пение) the second voice from the top is called the путь. Due to the lack of research in this subject, however it is still impossible to say conclusively whether the путь found in such polyphonic compositions has the same melodic characteristics as the unison chant melodies. The problem is compounded by the fact that Put' singing lost its significance in the course of the eighteenth century and was gradually forgotten. Those few melodies that were included in the Synodal chant-books were frequently designated as belonging to Znamenny Chant.

Demestvenny Singing[20] stands apart from the overall system of

церкви [The liturgical singing of the Orthodox Graeco-Russian Church], Vol. 1 — Теория и практика церковного пения [Theory and practice of church singing] (Moscow: 1886), p. 37n: "Знаменный путевой роспев своим происхождением обязан благочестию наших предков, которые не решались оставлять богослужения во время своих частых богомольных и дальних походов, неопустительно отправляли божественную службу, вечерню, утреню полунощницу и пр. Вместе с тем, благоговея к храму и его принадлежностям (утвари, облачениям, и пр.) они не решались в дороге или в пути, употреблять старый осмогласный роспев, как существенную принадлежность храма и его клироса, и для пения в путевом богомолении своем составляли особый осмогласный роспев, который от своего путевого или дорожнаго употребления и получил название путевого роспева."

[19] V. Beliaev, Древнерусская музыкальная письменность [Ancient Russian musical notation] (Moscow: 1962), p. 56.

[20] Concerning Demestvenny Singing and its notation, see: Johann v. Gard-

Russian liturgical singing, because it does not follow the system of eight tones. It was primarily used in those instances when the liturgical books did not prescribe a particular tone (usually hymns of the ordinary). On especially festive occasions it was also used for certain hymns that ordinarily were supplied with a designation of a tone (e.g., festal propers). Demestvenny Singing is first mentioned in fifteenth-century sources, although undoubtedly it originated earlier. Actual written monuments, however, date from the second half of the sixteenth century. The singing is notated in a special staffless notation with neumatic signs taken partly from stolp notation and partly from Put' Chant, while still other signs are unique to Demestvenny Singing.

The term *demestvenny* comes from *domestik* (δομέστικος; доместик, also spelled демстик, демественник), the leader of a choir or group of singers. The explanation given by Razumovskii—that Demestvenny Singing was a type of "domestic singing" to be used in the home [21]—again is erroneous, since all available evidence points to its use as liturgical singing in the church building itself. What Razumovskii interpreted as *cantus domesticus* is more correctly translated as *cantus arte domesticorum*, i.e., the singing art of the domestiks. Further evidence from liturgical books suggests that Demestvenny Singing was primarily employed on festive, solemn occasions.

Demestvenny Singing was performed both in unison and polyphonically, particularly in the seventeenth and eighteenth centuries, when scores containing up to four voices became common. [22] In these scores the top voice (or sometimes, the bottom) was labelled демество. Neither the unison nor the polyphonic variety of Demestvenny Singing has yet been adequately researched. The Synodal chantbooks, first published in 1772, contained very few Demestvenny melodies, only for a Pontifical Divine Liturgy. Beginning with the eighteenth century Demestvenny Singing began to lose its importance, and by the end of the century was almost entirely replaced by choral part-singing in the Western European style. Only the Old Believers have maintained the monophonic form of Demestvenny Singing to this day.

As was already mentioned above, beginning with the middle of

ner, *Das Problem des altrussischen demestischen Kirchengesanges und seiner linienlosen Notation* (Munich: Verlag Otto Sagner, Serie "Slavistische Beiträge," 1967).

[21] D. Razumovskii, Церковное пение. . . , Vol. 2, p. 180.

[22] E.g., a seventeenth-century MS in the Library of the British Museum, Add. 30063, "Hymnal in Russian."

the seventeenth century, canonical chants began to be performed in two, three, or four voices, rather than in unison, with increasing frequency. In the nineteenth century and particularly at the start of the twentieth, there appeared a large number of artistic arrangements and polyphonic settings of the canonical chants, for both mixed and male or female choirs, which preserved the canonical melodies intact while surrounding them with other voices. Insofar as these settings or harmonizations preserve the original melodies, they may be placed in the category of canonical singing.

In addition to the six systems of chant discussed above, it is necessary to mention yet one more system of liturgical singing, which occupies a middle ground between the *rospevy* (chants) and the *napevy* (melodies, tunes), and between canonical and non-canonical singing in general. This is the so-called Common Chant (обычный роспев, also referred to as обычный напев or обиходный —obikhod— роспев/напев). In one sense Common Chant can be seen as a complete system of liturgical singing, containing melodies for all hymnographical groups. In another sense, however, it lacks the unified character of other chant systems, being composed of an unsystematic conglomeration of greatly simplified and abbreviated melodies from various other chants, including some melodies of unknown origin. The polyphonic (harmonized) versions of Common Chant even include free compositions, which, as a result of frequent, almost daily use in services, have come to be regarded as canonical.

Common Chant originated from certain canonical chants and their local variants that were used daily in monasteries, parish churches, and especially, in the Imperial Court Cappella of St. Petersburg. At first it was transmitted by oral tradition, but beginning in 1848, it was transcribed and arranged for four-voice mixed choir under the guidance of the director of the Imperial Cappella, A. F. L'vov.[23] Once it was codified in this manner, the Common Chant (from then on also known as the Court Chant—придворный напев) was propagated all over Russia through L'vov's energetic administrative measures, and came to be employed not only for daily services when only a small number of singers were available, but also for festive services sung by large choirs.

Since this chant was neither approved nor censured by the Holy Synod for use in services, it must be classified as semicanonical singing: on one hand, it follows the indications of the Typikon to perform certain hymns in particular tones, while on the other hand, the

---

[23] I. Gardner, Алексей Феодорович Львов (Jordanville, New York: Holy Trinity Monastery, 1970), p. 47ff.

melodies from the tones have been greatly abbreviated and unsystematically juxtaposed (e.g. the heirmoi of one tone from Greek Chant; another tone, from Znamenny Chant; a third, from Kievan Chant, etc.). Moreover, for the purposes of harmonization many melodies have been simplified to fit more conveniently into a harmonic scheme, to the point where all melodic features are replaced by homorhythmic recitative on a few chords, with simple cadential formulae. During the nineteenth century this semi-canonical singing virtually supplanted the more correct canonical melodies in the practice of Russian church choirs.

A very large place in the liturgical singing of the present-day Russian Church is occupied by non-canonical singing—hymns whose texts are always canonical, but whose musical setting may be canonical or non-canonical, sanctioned for the liturgy through long-term usage. Non-canonical singing consists of freely-composed choral hymns on liturgical texts, as well as single-voiced melodies of unknown origin (or freely composed) that are not included in liturgical chant-books, and the polyphonic settings of such melodies.

It is difficult to establish a clear dividing line between canonical and non-canonical choral singing in the Russian Church. For such a classification there exists no reliable criterion: as a result of the introduction of polyphonic choral singing in the Western European style during the mid-seventeenth century, and its extraordinary development in the nineteenth century, the distinction between liturgical singing and secular vocal/choral music became less and less clear. The criterion for what was "churchly" or "unchurchly" came to be extremely subjective and open to endless argumentation. It appears, however, that one objective criterion may be suggested: the degree to which a freely-composed work approaches the spirit and character of the canonical models and fulfills the requirements of liturgical practice.

One other category of non-canonical singing yet remains to be mentioned: free compositions on liturgical texts or, more frequently, on texts from the psalms freely selected by the composer, which most properly should be termed *paraliturgical* singing. Paraliturgical compositions are usually performed at certain times during the Divine Liturgy, such as during the communion of the clergy (not to be confused with the Communion Hymn prescribed by the Typikon), but are not specifically provided for in the Typikon. Occasionally, the texts of such compositions are selected from stichera, troparia, or heirmoi of a given feast, but the musical setting is entirely inappropriate for performance at the point in the liturgy where that text would normally appear in the order of service. Like other types of

non-canonical singing, paraliturgical compositions have been sanctioned for use in the liturgy by long-term custom.

The various systems that comprise the liturgical singing of the
Russian Church may be summarized in the following fashion:

Canonical Singing	Non-Canonical Singing
Chants (*rospevy*) based upon the principle of eight tones: 1. Znamenny Chant 2. Kievan Chant 3. Greek Chant 4. Bulgarian Chant 5. Put' Chant	1. Freely-composed melodies and free settings or harmonizations of canonical melodies that have been fundamentally altered by the composer 2. Paraliturgical compositions

Outside of the eight-tone system:
Demestvenny Singing

Categories within canonical singing:

    I. Contents of chant system

        A. Complete chants
        B. Incomplete chants

   II. Melodic characteristics

        A. Great chant
        B. Middle chant
        C. Little chant

  III. Melodies (*napevy*) within a chant system

        A. For stichera
        B. For troparia, kontakia, and sedalens
        C. For heirmoi of kanons
        D. For prokeimena, alleluias, and other short responses
        E. For hymns of the ordinary

The Notations of Russian Liturgical Singing

An extremely important clue to understanding the system of
Russian liturgical singing is the study of the history and development
of the various types of notations used throughout the centuries to

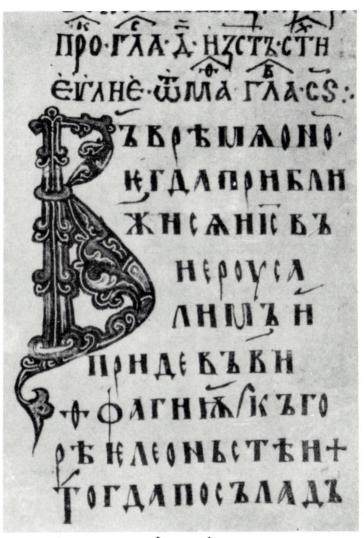

ILLUST. 1
Ekphonetic notation, eleventh-century Ostromirov Gospel, Russian
State Library, Number F. I. 5, fol. 140. (R. Palikarova Verdeil,
*La musique byzantine chez les Bulgares et les Russes du IXe au XIVe
siècle* [Copenhagen: E. Munksgaard, 1953], Pl. 1b).

ILLUST. 2
Kontakarion notation, eleventh-century Ustav of the Library of the
Synodal Press in Moscow, Number 142 (285, 1206). (M. Lisitsyn,
Первоначальный славяно-русский типикон [St. Petersburg: 1911],
appendix, p. 4).

ILLUST. 3
Stolp notation, twelfth-century Triodion of the Library of the New Jerusalem Monastery, Number 27. (M. Lisitsyn, Первоначальный славяно-русский типикон [St. Petersburg: 1911], appendix, p. 5).

ILLUST. 4
Square-note staff or Kievan notation, eighteenth-century Obikhod
(Moscow: Синодальная типография, 1794), p. 75.

set down the sacred melodies used in worship. For this reason it is necessary to discuss these notations, together with the sources in which they are found, without, however, entering into a great amount of detail, since this subject is treated extensively in other specialized literature.[24]

The most ancient written monuments of Russian liturgical singing date from the final years of the eleventh century or the first years of the twelfth century, thus falling within approximately one hundred years from the founding of the Russian Church. From that time to the middle of the seventeenth century, liturgical singing in Russia was notated by means of staffless neumatic notations. These notations were exclusively *vocal* notations, developed specifically for writing down liturgical singing. At no time were they used to set down instrumental music.

To express the contour of the melodic line, the notational signs were written directly above the verbal text, without any staff lines. The signs communicated the voice leading and the relative height and duration of the individual pitches as well as, at times, the manner of interpretation or execution of the given sign. The absolute level of the pitch did not have the same significance in this instance as it does in instrumental music (or in singing that is based upon the principles of instrumental music, such as present-day solo or choral singing). Rather, the height of the pitch was relative to the vocal range of a given individual singer and, therefore, was not fixed according to an absolute frequency. The staffless neumatic notation concerned itself primarily with intervallic relationships between individual tones and is thought to have been capable of expressing so-called "irrational" intervals or microintervals.[25]

Since the staffless vocal notations were used exclusively for setting down liturgical singing, they are sometimes referred to as "liturgical notations." This work, however, will adhere to the terminology employed by S. V. Smolenskii, who called them "singing notations" (певческие нотации), on the grounds that they were employed exclusively for the notation of vocal music.

The written musical monuments of Russian liturgical singing contain the following types of singing notations:

1. *Stolp notation* (столповое знамя), also commonly referred to as *hook notation* (крюковая нотация or simply крюки) or, more rarely, *znamenny notation*. As was mentioned earlier (n. 12 above),

---

[24] See n. 9 above.

[25] Intervals that cannot be expressed within the equally-tempered scale commonly used today. See J. B. Rebours, *Traité de psaltique* (Paris: Alphonse Picar & fils and Leipzig: Otto Harrassovits, 1906).

the latter term represents a tautology, since знамя means "sign" or "notation." The term *hook notation* is also ambiguous, since there are several different notations that contain signs of hook-like shape. In earlier times, all notations, including the later staff notation with square note-heads (Kievan notation) were called знамя. By contrast, the terms столповое знамя and столповая нотация precisely identify the system and type of notation as the one used for setting down Stolp (Znamenny) Chant.

This notation makes its appearance in the most ancient liturgical singing-books known today. While it underwent several stages of development, essentially the same notation was employed in Russia until the end of the seventeenth century; the Old Believers continue to use Znamenny Chant written in stolp notation to this day. While the problem of deciphering the most ancient forms of stolp notation still presents an unsolved task for the researcher, the later, seventeenth-century forms are easily decipherable and can be coordinated with present-day musical notation without any difficulty. Stolp notation was employed for almost all types of hymns, particularly heirmoi and stichera—hymns with a primarily syllabic melodic structure.

The detailed study of stolp notation reveals three basic varieties, which employ different methods for notating the relative pitch levels.

Type A employs cinnabar marks (киноварные пометы) to designate the relative height of the pitches. The marks consist of the initial letters of the words expressing the relationship: г—гораздо низко (quite low), н—низко (low), с—средним гласом (middle voice), м—мрачно (darkly), п—повыше (higher), and в—высоко (high). Moreover, there are additional signs, called признаки, consisting of dots and dashes written next to the neumes or directly upon them, in the same ink as the neumes themselves (i.e., black). This type of stolp notation, with two methods of designating relative pitch levels, serves as a point of departure for the study of older varieties of this notation. Its grammar is well-known, and deciphering it presents no difficulties. Arising after 1668 from Type B, Type A is the notation used by those Old Believers who have an ordained priesthood.

Type B notation also indicates the relative level of pitch by means of cinnabar marks, but contains none of the additional signs (признаки). It arose in the first half of the seventeenth century, or somewhat earlier, and is still employed today by the Old Believers who are priestless. This notation can be deciphered as easily as Type A.

Type C notation, also called беспометная нотация ("notation without marks") differs from Types A and B in that it does not employ cinnabar marks to designate relative pitch levels. Comparison of notations B and C shows that the actual neumes employed in both notations are identical; however, the neumes used in notation A differ slightly from those of notation C. Type C notation is not as easily decipherable as Types A and B, but it is the notation found in all of the oldest manuscripts written in stolp notation.

2. *Kontakarian notation* (кондакарное знамя) is another type of staffless notation found in a small number of the most ancient monuments of Russian liturgical singing (before the end of the thirteenth century). Sometimes it is found side by side with the oldest type of stolp notation (Type C), e.g., in the *Tipografskii Ustav*—the oldest manuscript of Russian liturgical singing, dating from the late eleventh or early twelfth century.[26] This notation differs markedly from stolp notation and, at the same time, is considerably more complex.[27] It was used primarily to notate kontakia (actually, only the first stanza—the kukulion), as well as some other hymns of the troparion-kontakion variety: hypakoe, sedalens and communion hymns. The hymns notated in kontakarian notation were collected in a book called the Kontakarion (Кондакарь), from which the notation received its name.[28]

While manuscripts containing stolp notation are fairly numerous (particularly after the fifteenth century), to this day there are only five known manuscripts written in kontakarian notation. The latest of these is thought to be the Uspenskii Kontakarion, which dates from 1207. Another manuscript, No. 777 from the former Moscow Synodal Library, dates from approximately the same period.[29] Metallov believes that it originates from the first half of the thirteenth century, but since the manuscript is not dated, it is impossible to say with certainty which of the two manuscripts is older.

As kontakarian notation fell from use in the late thirteenth or early fourteenth century, the kontakarian manuscripts lost their prac-

---

[26] V. Metallow, Русская симиография [Russian semeiography] (Moscow: 1912), Table IV.

[27] The terms кондакарное пение and кондакарное знамя were introduced by D. Razumovskii. See N. D. Uspenskii, "Византийское пение в Киевской Руси" [Byzantine singing in Kievan Russia] *Akten des XI. internationalen Byzantinisten-Kongresses 1958* (Munich: 1960), pp. 643-654.

[28] Constantin Floros, "Die Entzifferung der Kondakarien-Notation" in *Musik des Ostens*, Vol. 3 (Kassel: 1966) and Vol. 4 (Kassel: 1967); also published separately.

[29] V. Metallow, Богослужебное пение русской церкви в период домонгольский [The liturgical singing of the Russian Church in the pre-Mongol period] (Moscow: 1912), p. 212. The present-day signatures of these MSS, after their redistribution in the libraries of the USSR, are unknown.

tical significance. They remain, however, as valuable sources for the historical study of notation, as well as for the fields of liturgical archeology and Slavic philology. With time, the hymns contained in the Kontakaria come to be distributed in other liturgical books (Menaia, Triodia, Oktoechoi), either without neumes entirely or in stolp notation, omitting the characteristic instructions for execution that were communicated by kontakarian notation.

3. *Put' notation* (путевая нотация or путное знамя), a variant derived from stolp notation, arose in the very late fifteenth or early sixteenth century. The inventory of neumes in put' notation consists partly of contemporaneous stolp notational signs, as well as signs found only in the most ancient stolp manuscripts, which had fallen from use for many years and then suddenly reappeared in put' manuscripts. In addition, there are some characteristic shapes not found in any other system of notation. Put' notation, which is yet to be researched thoroughly, remained in use until the middle of the seventeenth century, whereupon it fell from use and was quickly forgotten.

4. *Demestvenny notation* (демественная нотация) is significantly more important among Russian staffless notations than put' notation. Like put' notation, however, it was derived from stolp notation and used specifically for writing down Demestvenny Singing. The inventory of neumes in demestvenny notation contains some signs from stolp notation, but these signs invariably assume a different musical or rhythmical meaning in the context of demestvenny notation. To these are added some signs from put' notation.[30] But specifically, demestvenny notation is characterized by complex signs that represent graphic combinations of stolp and put' neumes; these neumes are linked together forming what appear to be new signs.

Demestvenny notation was employed for writing down not only monophonic chant melodies, but also three- and four-voiced polyphonic scores, known as демественники. Manuscripts containing demestvenny notation began to appear in the third quarter of the sixteenth century, continuing to exist until the eighteenth century, when Demestvenny Singing fell from use in the ruling church. Only the Old Believers continued to use the notation to a limited extent. The deciphering of monophonic demestvenny chants dating from the seventeenth century presents no difficulty. A totally different situation exists, however, in the case of polyphonic demestvenny scores. The deciphering of these scores still presents a number of unsolved problems, primarily having to do with the vertical rhythmic coordination of the

---

[30] Johann v. Gardner, *Das Problem...*, pp. 142-160.

signs in adjacent voices, as well as the intervallic relationship between voices. The literal interpretation of the neumes, based upon the known relationships between cinnabar marks and the modern-day scale, often yield results that are both unperformable vocally and hardly tolerable to the ear. Whatever clues may have existed for the interpretation of polyphonic staffless demestvenny scores, they have yet to be rediscovered.[31]

Both put' and demestvenny notation were characteristic of the sixteenth and seventeenth centuries. Alongside stolp notation, which was, so to speak, universal, these notations were extensively used for setting down various types and systems of chants.

5. *Ekphonetic notation* (экфонетическая нотация) stands apart from the notations discussed above. In Russia it first appears in the Ostromirov Gospel, dating from 1056-1057. However, in this manuscript it appears only sporadically.[32] Properly speaking, this is not a singing notation, but rather, an intonational notation intended specifically for notating exclamatory reading (primarily of the Gospel). This type of reading is a combination of reading and singing: the middle of the phrase is recited on a single pitch, while the beginnings and ends of phrases contain brief, but fully sung melodic turns. Ekphonetic reading communicates a special musicality and expressiveness to the text, and is peculiar to liturgical singing, knowing no parallels in secular music. Although it was not intended for the singers, but rather for the cantors or the clergy—deacons, priests, or possibly bishops, who in certain cases read the Gospel themselves—, ekphonetic notation deserves mention as one of the important ways in which the musical element in the liturgy was notated. The use of ekphonetic notation continued in the Russian Church until the fifteenth century.[33]

[31] An attempt at deciphering *demestvenny* polyphonic scores was made by the Soviet musicologist S. Skrebkov, in Русская хоровая музыка XVII— начала XVIII века [Russian choral music of the seventeenth and early eighteenth centuries] (Moscow: 1969); however his method must yet be verified on the basis of original *demestvenny* sources located in the libraries of the USSR.

[32] N. Findeizen, Очерки по истории музыки в России [Essays in the history of music in Russia], Vol. 1, (Moscow-Leningrad: 1927), pp. 142-160; Остромирово Евангеліе 1056-1057 г. [The Ostromirov Gospel of 1056-1057], 2nd photolithographic ed. (St. Petersburg: 1889).

[33] Greek ekphonetic notation, which considerably antedates its Russian counterpart, has been investigated by the Danish scholar Carsten Høeg, *La notation ekphonétique*, Vol. 1, fasc. 2 (Copenhagen: Monumenta Musicae Byzantinae, Subsidia, 1935); see also, Findeizen, *op. cit.*, pp. 82, 85. Unfortunately, all attempts by the author to receive photocopies from the USSR of ancient Russian manuscripts from the twelfth-fifteenth centuries containing ekphonetic notation proved to be unsuccessful.

6. *Staff notation* (линейная нотация) or *Kievan notation* (киевское знамя) came into use in the Russian Church in the middle of the seventeenth century. This notation, employing square note-heads written in alto C-clef (more rarely, G- or F-clef) on a five-line staff, resembles the notation commonly used at that time in Western Europe for vocal as well as instrumental music.[34] In the southwestern part of Russia (present-day Ukraine) this notation began to be used for liturgical purposes as early as the end of the sixteenth century.[35] The Ukrainians used it not only for notating canonical liturgical singing, but also for non-liturgical sacred songs[36] and secular music. After the 1654 union of eastern Ukraine, including Kiev, with Muscovy, this notation, together with Western-style choral singing, was brought to Moscow by Kievan singing masters, thus acquiring the name of Kievan notation. Beginning with the second half of the seventeenth century and through the eighteenth century, this notation, which was much more convenient than staffless neumes for notating choral polyphony, began gradually to supplant the latter. The process was essentially complete by 1772, when the Holy Synod of the Russian Orthodox Church published the complete cycle of liturgical chants in square-note staff notation. Thus, the staffless neumatic notations fell out of use and were forgotten, not as a result of any specific prohibition, as is sometimes believed, but simply out of practical considerations.

In the last quarter of the eighteenth century, under the influence of secular Italian music and of Italian composers invited to the Russian Court, the modern round-note notation came into use. Thereafter, this notation become commonly employed for all types of choral and instrumental music. The Synodal liturgical singing-books, however,

[34] The present-day system of Gregorian neumes is different in that it uses a four-line staff and ligatures that express more than a single pitch; the Kievan five-line staff notation contained no ligatures.

[35] H. Pichura, "The Podobny Texts and Chants of the Suprasl Irmologion of 1601," *The Journal of Byelorussian Studies* 2 (1970), 192-221. After the *unia* of one faction of Orthodox in Polish-ruled Ukraine with the Roman Catholic Church in 1596, there began a very strong influence of Roman Catholic church music upon the liturgical singing of the Eastern Orthodox rite.

[36] S. V. Smolenskii, "О русской церковно-певческой литературе с половины XVII века до начала влияния приезжих итальянцев" [Russian church-musical literature from the mid-seventeenth century to the beginning of the influence of the invited Italians] Хоровое и регентское дело, no. 1 (January 1910): 6-7, no. 3 (March 1910): 57-58; S. V. Smolenskii, "Значение XVII века и его 'кантов' и 'псалмов' в области современного церковного пения так называемого 'простого напева' " [The significance of the seventeenth century and its 'kants' and 'psalms' in the area of the so-called 'common chant' of present-day church singing] Музыкальная Старина no. 5 (1911): 47-54.

continued to be published in square-note notation throughout the nineteenth and into the twentieth century. As a result, there arose the mistaken notion that the square notation was a specifically "liturgical" notation.

The survey of notations employed at various times in Russian liturgical singing would not be complete without mentioning a *numerical notation* (циферная нотация, цифирка) once employed by some church singers. Invented in the mid-nineteenth century by the Frenchman Chevé, it was extensively propagandized in late nineteenth-century Russia by S. V. Smolenskii, especially for use by village church choirs. In principle, this notation used numbers instead of notes on a staff to designate the various degrees of the scale. Melodies and choral scores could thus be printed without complicated and costly musical engraving. Instead of simplifying musical grammar, however, numerical notation turned out to be as difficult to master as common staff notation or even stolp neumes and was virtually abandoned by the first decades of the twentieth century.

There were also other staffless notations of minor importance, which were used for only a short time and in particular regions. One such notation was the *Kazan notation* (казанское знамя), which Oskar von Riesemann calls an experimental notation.[37] Other such notations are described by S. V. Smolenskii.[38] All of these notations date from before the end of the sixteenth century and had no practical significance for later types of notation.

The following chart summarizes the various systems of notation found in the liturgical singing of the Russian Church:

Century:	11/12	13	14	15	16	17	18
Stolp Notation C B A							
Kontakarian Notation							
Put' Notation							
Demestvenny Notation							
Ekphonetic Notation							

[37] Oskar v. Riesemann, *op. cit.*

[38] S. V. Smolenskii, О древне-русских певческих нотациях [Concerning ancient-Russian singing notations] (St. Petersburg: 1901), pp. 85-90, 99; D. Razumovskii, Церковное пение..., Vol. 1, p. 63; V. Metallov, Очерк..., p. 63; Oskar v. Riesemann, *op cit.*, p. 102.

Primary and Secondary Sources of Russian Liturgical Singing

By far the largest and most important group of sources related to the study of the history and development of both notation and liturgical singing itself consists of the liturgical singing-books containing various staffless notations and, beginning with the seventeenth century, staff notation as well. The most accessible sources for the canonical singing of the Russian Church are the square-note chant-books published by the Holy Synod of the Russian Orthodox Church. This series of books consists of five volumes:

1. *Common Hymns (Obikhod) in Staff Notation* (Обиходъ нотнаго пѣнія), in two parts: Part 1—All-Night Vigil, containing hymns for Vespers and Matins, with Sunday propers from the Oktoechos; and Part 2—Divine Liturgy. Both parts contain primarily the unchanging hymns of the ordinary for these services, but also certain propers for major feasts, taken from the Oktoechos, Heirmologion, and Feast-Days. A large number of chants are taken from the body of Znamenny Chant, but numerous examples of Kievan and Greek Chants are also included.[39]

2. *Oktoechos, that is, the Eight Tones in Staff Notation* (Октоихъ сирѣчь осмогласникъ нотнаго пѣнія), which contains all changeable hymns (stichera, troparia, heirmoi) of Sunday services, arranged in the order of service and according to the eight tones. The hymns are taken almost exclusively from the body of Znamenny Chant.

3. *Heirmologion in Staff Notation* (Ирмологій нотнаго пѣнія), which contains the heirmoi of all kanons, grouped by ode according

---

[39] The 1909 edition of the *Obikhod* was reprinted in 1966 by the Benedictines of Chevetogne, Belgium and Cureglia, Switzerland. There are other editions of the *Obikhod* that have little additional significance as sources of liturgical singing: (a) Сокращенный Обиходъ (Abridged *Obikhod*)—excerpted from the more complete *Obikhod*, and containing a smaller selection of hymns; (b) Учебный Обиходъ (Instructional *Obikhod*)—even more abridged, and adapted for instructional purposes, with exercises and explanations for learning square-note notation; (c) Пространный Обиходъ (Augmented *Obikhod*)—a very little-known edition that contains a much larger selection of hymns than the usual *Obikhod*, including hymns for private offices (Wedding, Burial, etc.); (d) Спутникъ псаломщика (The Cantor's Companion) — a chant-book containing all the most necessary hymns, excerpted from all of the square-note liturgical chant-books published by the Holy Synod; contains a preface that gives brief information concerning the structure of chants and instructions for reading square-note notation. (This theoretical portion, unfortunately, is quite out-of-date.) Offset reprint of the 2nd edition (St. Petersburg, 1916) published by the Holy Trinity Monastery, Jordanville, New York, 1959.

to the eight tones: the heirmoi of the first ode of every kanon in the first tone are grouped first, then the second odes in the first tone, etc., until all the tones have been presented. All of the melodies are taken from Znamenny Chant.

4. *The Feasts in Staff Notation* (Праздники нотнаго пѣнія), which contain all the propers (stichera, troparia, heirmoi) for nine of the twelve Great Feasts of the year, beginning with September.[40] The contents of *The Feasts* actually represent excerpts from the Menaion of the appropriate month, which have been supplied with musical notation for the convenience of the singers; also as a matter of convenience, the heirmoi of the kanons of the great feasts have been excerpted from the *Heirmologion*.

5. *Lenten Triodion* (Тріодь постная) and *Festal Triodion* or *Pentecostarion* (Тріодь цветная). The first part contains all of the propers and some of the hymns of the ordinary for Great Lent not found in the *Obikhod*, beginning with the fourth Sunday before Lent and ending with the Divine Liturgy of Great and Holy Saturday, arranged in the order of calendar days and services. The second part, the *Festal Triodion*, contains all of the propers beginning with Easter and ending with the first Sunday after Pentecost.[41] Most of the hymns are taken from Znamenny Chant.

A sixth volume, the *Trezvon* (Трезвонъ), was planned but never published. It was to have contained the propers for important feasts that are not included among the twelve Great Feasts (e.g., the Protection of the Mother of God, the Circumcision of Christ, the Feasts of St. Nicholas, Sts. Peter and Paul, etc.). The political events of 1917 prevented this volume from being published, and to this day, there is not a single printed *Trezvon* in existence; however, there are numerous *Trezvons* among the staffless handwritten monuments.

The various editions of the aforementioned books, beginning with 1772, differ from one another primarily in the layout of the

---

[40] The liturgical calendar year of the Church begins on September 1. The Great Feasts included in *The Feasts* are as follows: (1) Nativity of the Mother of God (September 8); (2) Elevation of the Cross (September 14); (3) Entrance of the Mother of God into the Temple (November 21); (4) Nativity of the Lord (December 25); (5) Theophany (January 6); (6) Meeting of the Lord (February 2); (7) Annunciation to the Mother of God (March 25); (8) Transfiguration of the Lord (August 6); and (9) Dormition of the Mother of God (August 15). The other three Great Feasts, Palm Sunday, the Ascension of the Lord, and Pentecost, are included in the Triodion and Pentecostarion cycles. Easter, the Feast of Feasts, occupies an entirely special position in the cycle of feasts.

[41] The Sunday of All Saints.

material and in the selection and versions of some chant melodies; these differences are insignificant, however. In general, the znamenny melodies contained in the printed books correspond to those found in handwritten chant-books of the late sixteenth, seventeenth, and eighteenth centuries, while the layout of the material follows that of the liturgical service-books without musical notation.

The series of chant-books edited and published under the auspices of the Holy Synod represent the final stage in the development of canonical singing in the Russian Church. The books contain the end result of various historical processes that began with the earliest neumatic manuscripts and ended in 1917 with the Russian Revolution.

Over the centuries, however, the contents of the handwritten chant-books did not remain uniform, due to changes in the amount and makeup of the hymnographical material that was sung: what these differences were, can be established by comparing the types and numbers of hymns found in later singing-books with those found in corresponding books of earlier periods. At various times in history, certain hymns were sung to an automelon (на самоподобен) and, therefore, were not supplied with musical notation of their own; the texts were contained in liturgical readers' books (see below).

The book that maintained the most consistent format and number of hymns over the centuries was the *Heirmologion*, although the number of heirmoi and actual kanons varied somewhat. Stichera were at one time collected in a separate volume called a *Sticherarion* (Стихирарь also written Стихираль),[42] a term that continued to be used into the seventeenth century. Eventually, however, the contents of the *Sticherarion* were included in a collection known as the *Singing Anthology* (Певческій сборникъ).[43]

Manuscripts bearing the title *Oktoechos* (Октоихъ, also Октай, Осмогласникъ) began to appear only in the fifteenth century.[44] Somewhat later, the *Obikhod* appeared, primarily as a component of the *Singing Anthology.*

---

[42] *Fragmenta Chiliandarica A. Sticherarium* (Copenhagen: Monumenta Musicae Byzantinae, 1957) is a Sticherarion composed of stichera that are now found in the Lenten and Festal Triodia. Virtually all of the hymns in this MS are notated with the most ancient type of stolp neumes. Among the stichera are also included the kontakion (kukulion) of Great Friday, the triodion of Great Friday (including melodies for the heirmoi as well as the troparia and sedalens). This MS contains the entire service for Great Friday, excluding the readings (pp. 27r.-57v.).

[43] The Певческій сборникъ may be likened to the Roman Catholic *Liber usualis* or the Protestant *Hymnal*, since it contains hymns for all occasions and services of the liturgical year.

[44] V. Metallov, Русская симиография, p. 41.

The *Singing Anthology* commonly began with a relatively complete Heirmologion, followed by an Oktoechos (actually, a Sticherarion of Sunday stichera, arranged according to the eight tones), which sometimes included Sunday troparia with their theotokia, gradual antiphons, the eleven Sunday exaposteilaria and Gospel stichera. The Oktoechos was followed by the Obikhod, which contained the hymns of the ordinary for Vespers and Matins. Usually, for each hymn in this section several different melodies were given (including settings in Put' Chant, either in put' notation or translated into stolp notation). Also this section contained melodic settings of sedalens, magnifications for various feasts, etc. Next appeared the hymns of Divine L:turgy and the propers of the twelve Great Feasts (stichera and, beginning with the seventeenth century, troparia as well). The next section of the *Anthology* consisted of the most important hymns from the Triodia (both Lenten and Festal), including unchanging hymns from the Liturgy of Presanctified Gifts. The *Anthology* concluded with various hymns for private offices (wedding, burial, etc.) and occasional services (consecration of a church, the service for the passing of summer and welcoming the New Year— September 1).[45]

In the period when Demestvenny Singing flourished (end of the sixteenth—beginning of the seventeenth centuries), there appeared some collections of both single-voiced and polyphonic Demestvenny Singing. Rather unsystematic in their contents, these collections, called *demestvenniki*, appeared both in score format and in the form of part books for single voices. Some of them bore extremely convoluted, grotesque titles, e.g.:

This book is called a mind-sharpener or tongue-loosener. It possesses a great depth of wisdom. Whoever

[45] Examples of such Сборники are MS slav. 5, of the Breslau State and University Library; the seventeenth-century MS, Mon. III, of the Bavarian State Library in Munich; See Johann v. Gardner, "Die altrussischen neumatischen Handschriften der Bayerischen Staatsbibliothek in München," *Welt der Slawen* 2 (1957): 322-328; Johann v. Gardner, "Die altrussischen neumatischen Handschriften der Pariser Bibliotheken," *Welt der Slawen* 3 (1958); Johann v. Gardner, "Die altrussischen Neumen-Handschriften in den Bibliotheken von Belgien und England," *Welt der Slawen* 4 (1961): 305-320. Certain such Сборники are called стихирарь or око дьячее; see S. V. Smolenskii, Краткий обзор крюковых и нотолинейных певчих рукописей Соловецкой библиотеки [A brief survey of the neumatic and staff manuscripts of singing found in the library of the Solovetskii Monastery] (Kazan: n.p. 1910), p. 55: "Стихерарь мѣсячный о Бозѣ начинаемъ мца сеп[тембрія] I. день же е[сть] дьячее око."

wishes to penetrate it with intelligent eyes will recognize that it holds the truth without darkness or confusion. It contains a collection of pieces in four parts. It is called Demestvenny Singing. It is set forth from the excellent oktoechos of the ancient and most wise rhetoricians. It is to the glory of God, the praise of the pious rulers and great hierarchs, and the heartfelt compunction of men.[46]

In the middle of the seventeenth century the first singing-books containing staff notation appeared in Muscovy. These can be divided into two categories: (a) manuscripts containing exclusively square-note Kievan notation, and (b) manuscripts written simultaneously in neumatic stolp notation and, underneath it, in Kievan staff notation—so-called *dvoznamenniki* (двознаменники; lit.: double-signed books).[47] Soon after their appearance, probably in the early eighteenth century, the *dvoznamenniki* fell from practical use, but not before nearly all of the hymns were transcribed in this parallel dual notation.

Many of the chant-books written exclusively in Kievan notation (category *a*) bear the title "*Heirmologion*" although in reality they are a type of *Singing Anthology*, containing not only hymns from the Heirmologion, but also from the Oktoechos, Obikhod, Menaion, and Triodion. The oldest manuscripts of this type are of Ukrainian origin (one, dating from 1652, is known, as well as another, possibly a little older).[48] Not long ago, the Suprasl' Heirmologion, dating from 1601, was found.[49] Similar manuscripts may still be awaiting discovery in the libraries of Poland and in libraries located on the territory that had belonged to Poland prior to World War II. Unfortunately, no full inventory of such manuscripts exists. While leading musicologists and paleographers of Russian liturgical singing are almost exclusively using materials located in the libraries of central Russia, the libraries

---

[46] "Книга глаголемая умноточецъ сии речь гласотечный. Имеетъ убо въ себѣ многоразумія глубину. Въ ню же кто умными очима приникнути желаетъ то не мрачно и неблазнено познаваетъ истину ея. Содержитъ въ себѣ собраніе четвероглаcныхъ вещей. Иже наричется демественное пѣніе. Изложено отъ прекраснаго осмогласія отъ древнихъ премудрыхъ риторь. Во славу Божію и въ похвалу благочестивымъ царемъ великимъ святителемъ и въ сердечное умиленіе человекомъ..."

[47] S. V. Smolenskii, Краткій обзор...," pp. 146-152; Oskar v. Riesemann, *op. cit.*, Table VIII.

[48] I. I. Voznesenskii, Церковное пение православной юго-западной Руси по нотно-линейным ирмологам XVII и XVIII веков [Church singing in Orthodox southwestern Russia from staff-notation Heirmologions of the seventeenth and eighteenth centuries], Vol. 1, 2nd ed. (Moscow: 1898), pp. 516.

[49] See n. 35 above.

of cities in western and southern Russia, as well as those of Eastern and Western Europe, are escaping their attention. Yet it is in the latter places that one must search for the origins of staff notation as it came to be used in Russian liturgical singing.

In 1700 the first printed edition of an Heirmologion with staff notation appeared in the city of L'vov, in western Russia.[50] This edition was followed by others (e.g., L'vov, 1709), containing some changes in format, including a later edition made by Uniates in the city of Pochaev. These early printed editions and manuscripts document the liturgical singing practiced by Orthodox and Uniates in the Ukrainian portion of the Polish kingdom in the first half of the eighteenth century.

Among historical sources pertaining to the knowledge of staffless notations, but which do not fall into the category of liturgical books, are the various instructional aids for the learning of these notations, the so-called "Alphabets" (Азбуки),[51] which began to appear in the late fifteenth or very early sixteenth century. Usually, such aids are found in the beginning, more rarely, at the end, of liturgical singing-books, and consist of a catalog that gives the shapes and the names of the neumes, without, however, any explanations or guides for interpreting or performing them. Later, in the seventeenth century, there began to appear meager, vague, and at times, equivocal discussions of how a given sign should be interpreted. Only in the middle and especially in the second half of the seventeenth century, there appear real textbooks of staffless notation, containing numerous examples from various hymns.[52]

Other important sources of liturgical singing are the numerous handwritten scores and part-books in Kievan notation dating from the seventeenth and eighteenth centuries. These manuscripts contain the earliest known attempts at arranging and harmonizing the ancient canonical melodies in polyphonic form, as well as free polyphonic compositions. It should be noted that these scores and part-books

---

[50] "Ирмолой си есть осмогласникъ, отъ старыхъ рукописныхъ экземпляровъ исправленный, благочиннаго же ради пѣнія церковнаго трудолюбіемъ іноковъ общежительныя обители святаго Великомученника Христова Георгія, въ катедре епископской Львовской, новотипомъ изданный року Божія 1700, мѣсяца октоврия въ 9-й день"; see D. Razumovskii, Церковное пение..., Vol. 2, p. 192; I. I. Voznesenskii, Церковное пение..., p. 6, n. 3.

[51] Johann v. Gardner and Erwin Koschmieder, *Ein handschriftliches Lehrbuch...*, Vol. 1, Prolegomena, p. XXIII; Johann v. Gardner, *Das Problem...*, pp. 31, 24-27, 177-270, and Tables.

[52] The best-known MS of this type was edited and published by S. V. Smolenskii, Азбука знаменнаго пѣнія....

also contained two-, three-, and four-voice sacred and secular songs, which were occasionally used for the setting of liturgical texts.

There is as yet no general catalog of ancient Russian manuscripts, written either in staffless or staff notation, found in the libraries of the USSR and other countries. Metallov and Uspenskii list only the most ancient and valuable manuscripts in their works on liturgical singing.[53] Very little is known, however, about manuscripts dating from the sixteenth century onward, although such manuscripts are found in great numbers in the libraries of the Soviet Union. The most extensive collection of such manuscripts was made by S. V. Smolenskii at the Moscow Synodal School of Church Singing: the catalog included 436 titles and 734 volumes.[54] After the Synodal School was abolished, following 1917, the collection came to be housed in other libraries and manuscript repositories in the USSR.

Libraries in the Western world, as well as certain private collections, also contain manuscripts of ancient Russian liturgical singing, none older, however, than the sixteenth century. For these manuscripts as well, there is no comprehensive catalogue. Only some of the largest libraries in Western Europe have partial descriptions of such manuscripts.[55] The search for other manuscript sources is made difficult by the lack of appropriate information in the library catalogs, as well as by a lack of systematized classification: in some instances, such manuscripts are classified in the Slavic section, while in others, in the musical section.[56] The time has come for a complete catalog

---

[53] V. Metallov, Богослужебное пение..., pp. 189--232; V. Metallov, Очерк..., p. XV; V. Metallov, Русская симиография..., pp. 71-108; N. D. Uspenskii, Древне-русское певческое искусство [The ancient-Russian art of singing], (Moscow: Музыка, 1965), p. 214.

[54] V. Metallov, Синодальное училище церковного пения в его прошлом и настоящем [The Synodal school of church singing in its past and present] (Moscow: 1911), pp. 132-133.

[55] See n. 45 above; also, Johann v. Gardner, "Ein neuerworbenes altrussisches Neumen-Triodion der Bayerischen Staatsbibliothek München," Welt der Slawen 5 (1960); Johann v. Gardner, "Russische Neumen-Handschriften der Bibliothek des Päpstlichen Orientalischen Instituts in Rom," Welt der Slawen 8 (1963); Sava Stela, "Trezvon-ul slav de la biblioteca akademiei republicii socialiste România (mss. slave nr. 771 si 772)," Studii si cercetari de istoria artei. Seria teatru, muzica, cinematografie 14 (1967), 59-69.

[56] A catalog might specify that a given MS is supplied with musical notation, but which notation—neumatic or staff—will not be indicated. Sometimes catalog descriptions are simply inaccurate: e.g., an Heirmologion dating from the end of the sixteenth-beginning of the seventeenth century, containing stolp notation of Type C, MS No. 11260 of the Royal Library of Brussels, is listed as being written in Slavonic and Tatar language. Upon examination, it turned out that the cataloger mistook the stolp notational signs for Tatar

to be compiled and published, which would include precise information and description of all manuscripts pertaining to ancient Russian liturgical singing found in the libraries of the entire world. Such a task would involve several specialists in different fields, and would require several years to accomplish.

It is surprising and unfortunate that many Russian scholars investigating ancient Russian liturgical texts completely ignored the musical notation, even when the texts were found in manuscripts with neumes, and centered their attention exclusively on the literary texts.[57] The impression is that they scorned the musical element and only recognized the significance of the verbal text. But in liturgical poetry the verbal element is very closely linked with the musical element, particularly in such cases as stichera sung to an automelon (e.g., the stichera in praise of Sts. Boris and Gleb) or kanons, in which the metric and melodic structure of the troparia must coincide with that of the heirmos. It is obvious that the poet's text must have been based to a certain extent on a given musical form. In general, many of the hymns composed on Russian soil must have had their musical and verbal components composed nearly simultaneously. Thus it would appear that the study of such monuments should be of interest to researchers in many other branches of knowledge dealing with the Eastern Slavs, and not only to musicology or linguistics.

Since liturgical singing is one of the forms of worship, generated and regulated by the order and structure of worship, one of the important resources for the study of this sacred art is the liturgical service-books of the Russian, as well as Greek and other Orthodox churches. These books fall into two categories: (1) *Singers' books* (певчие книги), books in which the verbal text is supplied with some form of musical notation, e.g., the Synodal chant-books discussed above, and (2) *Readers' books* (четьи книги), also known as *canonarchs' books* (канонаршия книги or, in distorted form, конархистные). While in these books the verbal text is not supplied with

writing! See Johann v. Gardner, "Die altrussischen Neumen-Handschriften in den Bibliotheken von Belgien und England..." pp 306-307.

[57] E.g., D. IU. Adamovich, Жизнь святых мучеников Бориса и Глеба и службы им [The lives of the Holy Martyrs Boris and Gleb, and services in their honor] (Petrograd, 1916), p. 137, gives the stichera to Sts. Boris and Gleb found in MS No. 589 of the Moscow Synodal Library, dating from 1157 (or 1152), only in the form of verbal text, without even mentioning the fact that these stichera are supplied with the most ancient type of stolp notation. For facsimiles of this MS, see V. Metallov, Русская симиография..., Tables XXV-XXVI.

musical notation of any kind, the fact that the hymns had a designation of a tone indicates that they are intended to be sung. These books
were used by the canonarch to prompt the singers, who then rendered
the text in musical form. The verbal text in these books was divided
into phrases, either by asterisks, or, in the older handwritten books,
by dots placed higher in the line of text than normal periods. Thus,
the canonarch already had a proper division of the text, in accordance
with the prescribed melody.

The discussion below will focus on some of the other liturgical
books that have a direct relationship to the musical aspect of worship.
One special group of such books consists of manuscripts intended
for ekphonetic reading (*lectio solemnis*); in some instances these
manuscripts contain ekphonetic notational signs. In general, the only
Russian lectionaries known to contain occasional ekphonetic signs
are those containing readings (pericopes) from the Gospel,[58] both
in the *aprakos* format and the *tetroevangelium* format.[59] The oldest
such manuscripts are the Ostromirov Gospel and the Kuprianov folios,
both dating from the eleventh century, while the latest is a Tetroevangelium from 1519.[60] Overall, however, there are very few Russian
manuscripts containing ekphonetic signs.

Another important category of liturgical books that serve as a
source for the history of liturgical singing is the typika (sing.: typikon;
типіконъ, сирѣчь уставъ церковный, also known as the обиходникъ).[61] These books contain not only the instructions for the order of
various services, but also indications and prescriptions concerning the
reading and singing of texts belonging to the yearly, weekly, daily, and
Triodion cycles. Occasionally, typika specify the manner or style in
which a given hymn is to be performed: e.g., by combined choirs, by a
soloist, slowly, quickly, etc. The texts of the most important hymns or
hymns performed only on particular occasions are sometimes given

[58] In the Greek tradition, lectionaries containing readings from the Epistles,
as well as the Old Testament—the Prophetologion (Russ.: паремийник)—
are supplied with ekphonetic notation.

[59] In the *aprakos* format, the texts are arranged according to the readings
throughout the liturgical calendar year, irrespective of the Evangelist or the
order of chapters. The *aprakos*-format Gospel begins with the reading at
the Divine Liturgy of Easter (John 1:1-17). In the *tetroevangelium* format,
the texts are arranged in order of the Evangelists (Matthew, Mark, Luke, and
John), without regard for the liturgical usage. In Gospels of the *tetroevangelium* format that are intended for liturgical use, the individual readings are
marked with an asterisk and the designation зач in a footnote.

[60] See n. 32 above.

[61] Not to be confused with the later (approximately sixteenth century
onward) liturgical chant-book called the Обиходникъ, or Обиходъ.

in full, and, in the most ancient typika, are even supplied with musical notation. One example of such a book is the *Tipografskii Ustav*, a Kievan typikon from the late eleventh or early twelfth century. There are many typika that contain specific rules of monastic life, as well as a monthly calendar of commemorations (Menologion; мѣсяце-словъ). The full investigation of such manuscripts lies more properly in the area of liturgics and liturgical archeology.[62] To the musicologist these sources are important insofar as they contain information concerning the order and performance of hymns, or texts supplied with neumes for musical performance.

Quite important in this regard are the typika of large and ancient cathedrals, such as the Moscow Cathedral of the Dormition or the Novgorod Cathedral of St. Sophia,[63] and those of ancient monasteries; such typika are called *chinovniki* (чиновники). The *chinovniki* contain descriptions of local customs with respect to the order of services and styles of singing. There are comments about particular chants and melodies used on special occasions, specifications regarding the division of hymns between two choirs and other styles of performance, as well as information concerning colors of vestments, liturgical actions, etc.

These ancient Russian *chinovniki* have been only partially researched. At the same time, a detailed study of them can yield much new information regarding the history and evolution of liturgical singing in Russia. But all of these monuments are located in libraries within the USSR and are not readily available to the Western researcher.

All of the sources mentioned thus far have pertained specifically to the study of the melodic forms of liturgical singing and its practical performance. Another aspect of the history of Russian liturgical

---

[62] See, e.g., M. Skaballanovich, Толковый Типикон [The explanatory Typikon] (Kiev: 1910); M. Lisitsyn, Первоначальный славяно-русский типикон [The first Slavic-Russian Typikon] (St. Petersburg: 1911); I. D. Mansvetov, Церковный устав (типик), его образование и судьба в греческой и русской церкви [The Church Typikon, its formation and development in the Greek and Russian Church] (Moscow: 1885).

[63] A. Golubtsov, Чиновник Новгородскаго Софийскаго собора [The *chinovnik* of the Novgorod Cathedral of St. Sophia] (Moscow: 1899; A. Golubtsov, Чиновники Московскаго Успенскаго собора и выходы патриарха Никона [The *chinovniki* of the Moscow Cathedral of the Dormition and the pronouncements of Patriarch Nikon] (Moscow: 1908); A. Golubtsov, Соборные чиновники и особенности службы по ним [The *chinovniki* of the cathedrals and the peculiarities of services according to them] (Sergiev Posad: 1907); A. Golubtsov, Чиновники Холмогорского Преображенского Собора [The *chinovniki* of the Kholmogory Cathedral of the Transfiguration] (Moscow: 1903).

singing, however, focuses on the general development of the art, taking into consideration various historical and sociological factors that affected its course through the centuries. Many of the aforementioned musical manuscripts and instructional materials contain informative forewords that are of great interest for this broader, purely historical approach.[64]

In addition to liturgical books, ancient Russian chronicles (летописи) and similar writings contain important material for the history of liturgical singing. Unfortunately, the chronicles themselves contain remarkably little mention of liturgical singing. More information is found in the official acts of the councils of the Russian Orthodox Church, e.g., the Stoglav Council of 1551 [65] and the Council of 1667-68. Other valuable material is found in historical acts and documents located in Soviet archives, the collected acts of the Holy Synod (from the eighteenth through the first two decades of the twentieth century), various official and semi-official newspapers and periodicals, such as the Церковные ведомости, the journal of the Holy Synod published from 1886 to 1917, and various diocesan newspapers. Equally valuable are the correspondence and official resolutions of leading hierarchs who were active in maintaining the quality and order of liturgical singing in their dioceses.[66]

Other historical materials include accounts of travels in Russia by individuals from other countries who address themselves to church singing and liturgical practices. Valuable information is found in the description of Patriarch Makarios of Antioch's journey to Moscow in 1654, made by Deacon Paul of Aleppo, who accompanied the Patriarch. Deacon Paul took particular notice of church customs and liturgical singing.[67] Other valuable observations were made of church singing in Kiev in the second half of the seventeenth century by Johannes Herbinius.[68]

---

[64] V. M. Undol'skii, Замечания для истории церковного пения в России [Comments on the history of church singing in Russia] (Moscow: 1846), pp. 19, 34; S. V. Smolenskii, "Музыкальная грамматика Николая Дилецкого," Proceedings of the Общество Любителей Древней Письменности (1910), 5-57.

[65] Стоглав (Moscow: 1890).

[66] Собрание мнений и отзывов Филарета митрополита Московского и Коломенского [The collected opinions and testimonials of Filaret, Metropolitan of Moscow and Kolomna] (St. Petersburg: Синодальная типография, 1885-1887). This work contains very interesting and important material concerning the development of Russian liturgical singing in the mid-nineteenth century.

[67] Russian trans. in Чтения в Императорском Обществе Истории и Древностей Российских при Московском Университете, Book 4 (1897).

[68] Johannes Herbinius, Religiosae Kyoviensis cryptae sive Kyovia subterranea, (Jena: 1675).

To this category also belong various memoirs dealing with liturgical singing, either in passing or specifically. Such memoirs present particularly valuable information for the last period of the second epoch, i.e., the nineteenth and early twentieth centuries.[69]

[69] "Записки Алексея Феодоровича Львова" [The notes of Aleksei Feodorovich L'vov], Русский Архив, book 2, ser. 3 and 4 (1884), 225-260.

CHAPTER IV

*Periodization of
Russian
Liturgical
Singing*

Before turning to the actual history of Russian liturgical singing, it is important to examine several different points of view from which that history has been approached by past historians.

The two most significant historians of church singing in Russia, Dimitrii Razumovskii and Vasilii Metallov, as well as the lesser historians, A. Ignat'ev and D. Allemanov, who followed the former in many details,[1] begin their histories of Russian church singing with accounts of liturgical singing among Christians in general, from the first centuries of Christianity. They then deal briefly with the liturgical singing of the Western Church until the time of the Schism of 1054, and with the singing of the Church of Byzantium until the thirteenth or fourteenth century. The following chapters are then devoted exclusively to the history of Russian church singing, beginning with the year 988.

At the time these works were written, such an approach to the history of church music fulfilled a necessary function, since there existed no other general histories in the Russian language of Christian church singing. Furthermore, the authors considered it particularly important to prove and underscore the derivation of Russian church singing from that of the Byzantine Church and the early Christian Church in general.

Today, the Western reader has at his disposal a wealth of specialized literature in English and other Western European languages dealing with the liturgical singing of the Western Church, as well as detailed monographs concerning various aspects of Byzantine church singing. For this reason it would be redundant to begin the present historical survey with the singing of early Christendom. Rather,

---

[1] D. V. Razumovskii, Церковное пение в России [Church singing in Russia] 3 vols. (Moscow: 1867-1869); V. M. Metallov, Очерк истории православного церковного пения в России [Essay on the history of Orthodox church singing in Russia] 1st ed. (Moscow: n.p. 1893) and subsequent editions; A. A. Ignat'ev, Богослужебное пение православной русской церкви с конца 16-го до начала 18-го века [The liturgical singing of the Orthodox Russian Church from the end of the sixteenth to the beginning of the eighteenth century] (Kazan: 1916); D. Allemanov, Курс истории русского церковного пения [A course of history of Russian church singing] Vol. 1 (Moscow: 1912), Vol. 2 (Moscow: 1914).

it will begin with the time when the Orthodox Church was first established among the Eastern Slavs, i.e., immediately after the baptism of Russia under Prince Vladimir of Kiev, which took place in 988 or 989.

By this time there already existed a fully developed system of liturgical singing and liturgical order, both in the Eastern Byzantine Church and in the Western Roman Church, a system that had evolved over a period of eight or nine centuries. The Slavs, who accepted the Byzantine rite, thus received a complete liturgical scheme, complete with rules and traditions of liturgical practice. The continued development of church singing among the Russians ran parallel, in part, to that of the Greek Church; certain changes in the liturgical practice of the Greeks were adopted by the Russians, while other innovations and variants arose locally in the Russian Church.

As in Byzantium, the civic life in Kievan Russia immediately following the Christianization of the Slavs became "inseparable, yet independent" of church life. At the same time, as certain layers of Kievan society accepted many elements of contemporary Byzantine culture and civilization, if not fully, at least partially Orthodoxy and Byzantine Orthodox church culture became powerful forces in shaping an indigenous Russian culture in general and Russian church-musical culture in particular.

The language used in the liturgy at that time was quite close to the vernacular and was understood by all. This strengthened the influence of the Church on daily life and tightened the bond between the Church and the secular rulers, at least in individual feudal principalities. As time went on, the rate of development of the vernacular overtook the rate at which the liturgical language changed, resulting in an archaic sacral language that, nevertheless, did not cease to be comprehensible to a majority of the people. Ideas expressed in the texts could be grasped easily, especially when the texts were linked with melodies.

Thus, liturgical singing became a very important aspect of Russian culture. It is noteworthy that from the eleventh until the seventeenth century there is not a single written monument of secular or non-liturgical music to be found. From the point of view of general music history, it can be said that the documentable history of Russian music begins with Russian liturgical singing. However, as has been pointed out earlier, liturgical singing has its own aesthetic laws and styles of performance, which are inseparable from the liturgy itself. And hence, the history of this sacred art is dependent upon factors other than those regulating secular music or folk music. Even in times when sacred singing came into very close contact with secular music and was, in fact, strongly influenced by the latter, as in the late eighteenth and nineteenth centuries, it still maintained its own course of development. Therefore, it must be viewed as a separate field of investigation with its own specific research problems.

The very fact that Orthodox Christianity in its initial stages was a cult imported into Russia from outside, suggests that the musical forms belonging to it were different from the pagan forms that had theretofore existed. But inasmuch as the Christian culture was a new and foreign (non-Slavic) element that had been introduced into an already established pagan society, it was equally possible for pagan ways to influence the newly-imported Christian culture. As a result of this interaction, the history of Russian liturgical singing came to rest on different bases than the history of Russian secular and folk music.

Among the tasks facing the researcher in the field of Russian church singing is the exploration of these questions: What significant elements were borrowed, in the course of time, from other nations and other church cultures, and to what degree did these borrowings affect the development of the system and nature of Russian liturgical singing?

In spite of the fact that borrowed elements certainly exerted a transforming influence on Russian liturgical singing from time to time, it must be remembered that the development of liturgical singing remained within clear guidelines and traditions that were centuries-old: the order of worship, the various liturgical texts, and different ways of organizing the musical element—from psalmody and ekphonesis, which have remained unchanged, to canonical singing (chant), the more recent forms of which may be retrospectively traced to forms from ancient times. Within the context of continuing traditions of liturgical singing, there functioned the creative activity of hymnographers and master-singers, who introduced new forms and melodies into their art.

The following factors may serve as criteria for the division of the history of Russian liturgical singing into chronological periods:

1. Peculiarities of linguistic texts found in musical manuscripts. (The evolution of the language often brought with it the evolution of the melodic content.)

2. Differences in musical style and semiographic characteristics.

3. Development and evolution (and at times, devolution) of the liturgical order.

4. Political events that affected liturgical format and the liturgical arts.

The history of liturgical singing in Russia is quite complex. The characteristic features and prevailing factors affecting its nature were very diverse at different points in time. To attempt to base the nine-century-long history of this art on only one of the above criteria would lead to very questionable results. In addition to being affected by all of the aforementioned factors, church singing in Russia was influenced by a variety of forces from outside Russia.

In this regard, it is necessary to distinguish between influence and borrowing. "Influence" consists in the partial action of certain foreign elements upon an already existing cultural heritage or tradition of a given people, without changing that heritage in its totality or essence, or pushing it aside and replacing it with something altogether new. "Borrowing," on the other hand, represents a more or less complete adoption or transplantation of a foreign cultural heritage—the product of a foreign and differently directed spiritual orientation. At first, borrowing brings with it and establishes totally foreign forms; but with the passage of time, that which was borrowed becomes transformed according to the spirit and technical aptitudes of the borrowing nation, and begins to be viewed as part of the indigenous cultural heritage. Only in-depth analysis can reveal the elements that were originally foreign.

Borrowing and assimilation in no way reduce the value of the indigenous cultural heritage. Contact with other nations and their spiritual cultures frequently occurs imperceptibly and is assimilated unconsciously. A nation absorbs from a foreign culture only those things that answer to its spiritual needs at the time.

In general, it is impossible to draw any sudden or clear-cut chronological boundaries between the different periods in the history of Russian liturgical singing. While the divisions made below are based upon more or less datable characteristics, they serve only as orientation points for a systematic outline of history. Substantive changes in liturgical singing did not occur suddenly, but rather, over a certain period of time: elements characteristic of a given period began to occur episodically either before or after a certain arbitrary chronological boundary. It is obvious that an older generation of singers holds on to established forms and practices, and is slower to accept new forms, while the next generation is likely to adopt newer forms more readily. Thus a transition period occurs during which the old exists side-by-side with the new; between the various periods of history outlined below there can be observed transitional stages of approximately fifty years, during which characteristics of an older style gradually diminished and were replaced by new stylistic features.

The history of Russian liturgical singing can be divided into two major epochs of unequal duration. The essential distinction between them is based not only on stylistic and technical differences or types and styles of performance, but also on changes in ideology. In these two epochs there existed two fundamentally different conceptions concerning the essence of liturgical singing and its function in worship. The dividing line between the two epochs is quite clear: the years 1652-1654, when an almost revolutionary change occurred in Russian liturgical singing.

The first epoch, lasting from the Christianization of Russia to the mid-seventeenth century, may be termed the epoch of monophonic church singing, since throughout this period Russian liturgical singing was almost exclusively performed in unison (or in parallel octaves). Only towards the very end of this epoch can one speak of polyphony, and even so, polyphony that appears to be in no way related to the Western European polyphonic style.

The second epoch, from the mid-seventeenth century to the present day, may be called the epoch of polyphonic choral singing, during which Russian liturgical singing took on essentially the same stylistic features found in the mainstream of Western European choral polyphony.

This division into two epochs is found in the writings of both Razumovskii and Metallov: both call the first period the epoch of melodic singing (эпоха мелодического пения);[2] the second epoch is termed the epoch of "part"[3] singing (эпоха партесного пения) by Razumovskii,[4] while Metallov calls it the epoch of harmonic singing (эпоха гармонического пения).[5] Both authors agree with respect to the dates and major characteristics of each epoch; but the characteristics of individual periods within each epoch, especially of the second epoch, are not entirely clear in their works.

---

[2] D. Razumovskii, Церковное пение..., Vol. 1, p. 57.

[3] The Russian term партесное пение ("part" singing) arose from the russified form of the Latin word *partes* — parts. In its initial usage, the term was applied to any free composition or polyphonic arrangement of a chant melody that was actually composed and precisely notated, as opposed to being improvised by ear in the traditional fashion (see Chap. III, p. 102); the latter was referred to as простое пение — plain singing. Although some nineteenth-century writers on liturgical music applied this definition of "part" singing to all polyphonic choral music written after the mid-seventeenth century, more recent scholarly usage has restricted the term specifically to the Polish-Ukrainian style of the late seventeenth-early eighteenth century. The present work will adhere to the narrower definition of the term.

[4] D. Razumovskii, Церковное пение..., Vol. 2, p. 207.

[5] V. Metallov, Очерк..., p. 95.

Both Razumovskii and Metallov divide the first epoch on the basis of philological factors into three periods:

1. *The period of old true speech* (период старого истинноречия), which lasted from the ninth-tenth centuries to the fourteenth century. In this period the half-vowels ъ and ь were pronounced in the every-day spoken language and could therefore be sung as well. In the manuscripts of this period these letters are supplied with neumes, just as other vowels.

2 *The period of divergent speech* or *the period of khomoniia* (период раздельноречия ог период хомонии), which lasted from the fourteenth to the seventeenth century. During this time, ъ and ь lost the character of half-vowels in spoken language and became either completely silent or, in certain limited instances, fully voiced as vowels. In liturgical singing books, however, these letters continued to have neumes placed above them in every instance and therefore had to be vocalized: ъ as "o" and ь as "e." This resulted in a distortion of the pronunciation as well as, on occasion, the entire meaning of words. Because of the frequent verb-ending -хомъ, which now became vocalized as -хомо, this phenonmenon came to be known as хомония, *khomoniia*. A text that was sung differed markedly from one that was read, hence the term "divergent speech."

3. *The period of new true speech* (период нового истинноречия), which began with the liturgical and textual reforms carried out by Patriarch Nikon from 1652 to 1658. In this period, ъ and ь ceased to be vocalized as "o" and "e" when sung, and therefore, sung texts once more were pronounced the same as when they were read. Traces of *khomoniia* remained only in the singing of the priestless Old Believers.

In dividing the second epoch into periods, Metallov also agrees with Razumovskii; both divide the epoch into two periods. While Metallov, writing thirty years after Razumovskii, brings his history to the end of the nineteenth century, Razumovskii's work ends with the middle of the nineteenth century. Both historians employ the various foreign influences that came to affect Russian liturgical singing as the basis for characterizing the periods. Thus, they distinguish the following:

1. The period from the mid-seventeenth to the end of the eighteenth century, during which the Polish-Ukrainian influence was particularly strong, and

2. The period of Italian influence, which began at the end of

the eighteenth century and lasted approximately to the time when Razumovskii and Metallov were writing.

Another historian, A. V. Preobrazhenskii, divides the history of Russian liturgical singing into five periods: [6]

1. From the tenth through the fourteenth century.
2. From the fourteenth to the seventeenth century.
3. The seventeenth century.
4. The eighteenth century.
5. The nineteenth century.

Preobrazhenskii's criteria for dividing history into periods are different from those of Metallov and Razumovskii, so his chronology corresponds with theirs only in part. His fifth period is based primarily on biographical information about various church composers. Preobrazhenskii concludes his historical survey with the first decade of the twentieth century. But it is difficult to distinguish a clear system in his work: it has more the character of a survey, rather than a scholarly work.

The Soviet scholar N. D. Uspenskii, in his work Древнерусское певческое искусство (The Ancient-Russian Art of Singing),[7] covers the history of Russian liturgical singing from its origins to the end of the seventeenth century; thus, he includes the early period of polyphonic singing in the Western style. Uspenskii bases his system of history on the political history of early Russia, dividing it into three periods:

1. The period of Kievan Russia, from the tenth through the mid-twelfth century—the point in time when the principality of the Grand Prince of Kiev became fragmented into several feudal principalities and Kiev lost its significance as the capital city.

2. The period of smaller feudal principalities.

3. The period of the Muscovite state.

Concerning this type of division of church singing history, it should be pointed out that political changes in the administrative organization of the Russian state could not have had the same signifi-

---

[6] A. V. Preobrazhenskii, Очерк истории церковного пения в России [Essay on the history of church singing in Russia] (St. Petersburg: Санкт-Петербургское Регентское Училище, n.d.); since this work mentions the year of S. V. Smolenskii's death, 1909, it is reasonable to assume that it was published no earlier than 1910 and not later than 1914, when St. Petersburg was renamed Petrograd.

[7] (Moscow: Музыка, 1965).

cance for church singing as they did for political, economic, and social history. Throughout these changes the Church remained a single entity, forming a united metropolitanate (from 1589, a patriarchate) with several dioceses. The entire Church had a single liturgical language and liturgical order, and hence, a single body of liturgical singing (with minor local and regional variants) in all feudal principalities and dioceses. Since the unity of the Church was little affected by external political conditions, it appears that Uspenskii's basis for the division of Russian church singing into periods is not entirely appropriate.

The history of liturgical singing did follow a somewhat different course in the southwestern parts of the territory that once belonged to the Princes of Kiev—parts annexed by the Grand Duchy of Lithuania and the Kingdom of Poland (Belorussia, Western Ukraine, and Galicia). The history of church singing in these regions has not yet been satisfactorily researched. For this reason, beginning with the fourteenth century, the present survey of history will concentrate on liturgical singing in those areas that eventually developed into the Russian state. At the same time, it should be noted that the results of nearly four centuries of development in the southwestern regions of Russia played an extremely important, almost revolutionary role in the history of Russian liturgical singing after the mid-seventeenth century.

The history of church singing among the Old Believers, who in 1668 split off from the hierarchy of the Russian Orthodox Church as a result of Patriarch Nikon's liturgical reforms, has also not been thoroughly researched. In reality, however, the liturgical singing of the Old Believers contains very little that is new. It has merely been a continuation of the same kind of singing that had existed immediately prior to the schism. Thus, it may be said, that the Old Believers are still continuing the last period of the first epoch in the history of Russian church singing to this very day.

Since the appearance of the last comprehensive scholarly works on the history of Russian liturgical singing, sixty years have passed. (Uspenskii's aforementioned work unfortunately deals with only the first epoch and the very beginning of the second.) Today, many of the facts and conclusions that appear in those works require extensive re-examination and supplementation.

The essential differences between the first and second epochs of Russian liturgical singing as observed by Razumovskii and Metallov are so stark, that only slight modifications and additions, based on recent research, are required to the method by which these scholars arrived at their conclusions. As has already been noted, all written monuments of liturgical singing prior to the mid-sixteenth century are, without exception, monophonic. Manuscripts containing polyphony for two or more voices begin to appear only in the second half of the sixteenth century. But this polyphony is fundamentally different from contemporaneous Western European polyphony, since it is in no way based upon the principles of instrumental music.

These two characteristic phenomena—monophony and vocal polyphony of a unique character—are the two distinguishing features of the first epoch. Whether this early Russian polyphony was originally invented and developed on Russian soil by Russian singing-masters,[8] or was imported from elsewhere at a much earlier time is of secondary significance at this point. What is important is that it was entirely different from the polyphony that suddenly burst into Russian liturgical singing from the West in the middle of the seventeenth century.

The criteria that will be employed in the present work for dividing the first epoch into periods will be predominant types of singing found in extant written monuments of liturgical singing. On this basis the first epoch may be divided into four periods:

1. *The period of origins*, lasting from 988 to approximately the end of the eleventh century, i.e., from the baptism of Russia to the appearance of the first known manuscripts of liturgical singing written on the territory of the Russian metropolitanate in the Slavonic language. Since there are no written monuments from this period, any conclusions regarding church singing of this time must be based, at least in part, on conjecture.

2. *The period of Kontakarian Singing*, lasting from the end of the eleventh to the end of the thirteenth century, when, according to known written monuments, there coexisted two fundamentally different types of singing: (a) Znamenny Chant, with its characteristic staffless stolp notation, and (b) Kontakarian Singing, which also had its unique staffless notation. Since Kontakarian Singing is unique to this period, it may be used to identify the period by name, in spite of the fact that Znamenny Chant appeared to have been used more widely than the former. In terms of liturgical practice, this period is characterized by the use of the Constantinopolitan liturgical order. Cathedrals of this time used the order of the Great Church—τῆς μεγάλης ἐκκλησίας—the Cathedral of St. Sophia in Constan-

---

[8] V. M. Beliaev, "Раннее русское многоголосие" [Early Russian polyphony] in *Studia memoriae Belae Bartok sacra* (Budapest: 1956) pp. 327-336; English translation: pp. 307-326.

tinople, while monasteries employed the order of the Constantinople Monastery of the Studios. This period ended already in the thirteenth century; there are no known fourteenth-century monuments containing kontakarian notation.

3. *The period dominated by Znamenny Singing alone.* All written monuments from this period contain exclusively Znamenny Chant set down in stolp notation. At the same time, changes were made in liturgical practice, substituting the order of Jerusalem and the Mount Athos monasteries (Hagiopolitical-Hagiooritical order) for the Constantinopolitan order theretofore employed. The period extends from the beginning of the fourteenth to the beginning of the sixteenth century, at which time there began to appear other types of staffless notation (put' and demestvenny) alongside the prevailing stolp. On the basis of semeiography, the boundary between the third and fourth periods may be placed at the turn of the sixteenth century.

4. *The period of early Russian polyphony.* This period is characterized, first of all, by the appearance of new, heretofore non-existent notations and types of singing—put' and demestvenny—which were not necessarily performed monophonically. Also, in this period one finds the first mention of schools for church singers and organized choirs, as well as textbooks (азбуки) of stolp notation. The full flowering of this period occurred only towards the end of the sixteenth century, while events of the mid-seventeenth century brought about an abrupt halt both to this period and the entire first epoch.

The second epoch in the history of Russian liturgical singing is best characterized as the *epoch of Western-style choral singing.* The reason why Razumovskii's designation of this epoch as the *epoch of "part" singing* is inappropriate, is clear from note 3: it would be incorrect to label an entire epoch, which continues to this day, with a term that properly applies only to a limited period of the late-seventeenth and early-eighteenth centuries. Similarly, Metallov's designation of this epoch as the *epoch of harmonic singing* is not entirely accurate, since during this time, not only harmonic principles were employed in the composition of church singing, but also principles of complex counterpoint and imitative polyphony, both in free compositions and in polyphonic settings of ancient canonical melodies. The designation of this period as the *epoch of Western-style choral singing,* however, is most appropriate, since this period is indeed characterized by choral polyphony based upon commonly-practiced Western European principles of counterpoint, harmony, and formal structure. During the second epoch, Western-style compositional technique began to obscure and supplant the *word* and the heretofore zealously cultivated canonical melodies. As a result, the further development of the ancient Russian forms of liturgical singing, as well as early Russian polyphony, came to a halt.

While both Razumovskii and Metallov divide the second epoch into periods on the same principles and in an identical fashion, the present work suggests a different periodization. This is because at the time Razumovskii and Metallov were writing, the characteristics of the final periods suggested here had not yet become clearly established.

The criteria for dividing the second epoch into periods are the typical stylistic features that can be observed in polyphonic choral music of different times. These criteria are sufficient for this purpose, since by this time the liturgical order of the entire Russian Church had already become stabilized, remaining virtually the same until the present day. While social conditions in Russia did change radically during the second epoch, these changes affected only the quality of choral singing, but did not have a marked effect on the *essence* of liturgical singing. Rather, church singing was most affected during this time by various foreign influences, which, following the general evolution of musical style in Western Europe, often became decisive factors in determining the prevailing composition technique and style of Russian church singing.

The second epoch may also be divided into four periods:

1. *The period of Polish-Ukrainian influence*, marked by the florid, often poly-choral "part" (партесный) style, as well as the simpler "kant" (кантовый) style inspired by the Protestant chorale. This period extends from the second half of the seventeenth century to the mid-eighteenth or slightly later. Beginning with this period, liturgical singing ceases to be considered as a form of worship itself and begins to be viewed as *music* introduced into church services.

2. *The period of Italian influence*, especially Italian-style choral polyphony. This period was relatively brief, lasting from the middle of the eighteenth through the first third of the nineteenth century.

3. *The period of German influence*, during which Romantic and pietistic feelings introduced a strong emotional element into church singing. In this period church singing came under increasing regulation by secular authorities, headed by the St. Petersburg Imperial Court Cappella in the person of its directors. According to their personal taste, these directors decided upon the style of new compositions for liturgical use, including the very makeup of melodies for the church tones. For this reason, this period may properly be called

the *Petersburg period.* This period also included the first scholarly investigations into the history, paleography, and semeiography of Russian liturgical singing. The results of these investigations were partially responsible for the fourth period of the second epoch. The third period extended from the second third until the end of the nineteenth century.

4. *The period of the Moscow School,* which began at the very end of the nineteenth century and is still continuing today. This period is characterized by the search for new ways of liberating Russian liturgical singing from foreign influences and borrowings that strongly manifested themselves during the preceding three periods of the second epoch, particularly in the third period. The new directions were marked by a return to the indigenous and thoroughly Russian canonical melodies, and the application to those melodies of the latest achievements of Russian compositional technique in conjunction with the unique feeling and spirit of Russian folk music.[9] During this period, the position of leadership in church singing shifted from St. Petersburg and its Imperial Cappella to the Moscow Synodal Choir and Church Choir School. By the Russian Revolution of 1917, the art and culture of Russian liturgical choral singing had reached its highest stage of development. The political events of 1917 and the years following, however, effectively interrupted all further development of this art, preventing the transference and nurture of the liturgical singing tradition. There are no reliable sources that can authoritatively provide information concerning the state of liturgical singing on the territory of the USSR after 1917

[9]The inherent features and principles of Russian folk heterophony were described by A. D. Kastal'skii in Особенности русской музыкальной системы [The peculiarities of the folk-Russian musical system] (Moscow and Petrograd: Музсектор Госиздата, 1923).